Dancing Mama

Juliana Richmond

TRAFFORD

USA ▪ Canada ▪ UK ▪ Ireland

Note for Librarians: A cataloguing record for this book is available from Library and Archives
Canada at www.collectionscanada.ca/amicus/index-e.html
ISBN 1-4251-0385-5

Printed in Victoria, BC, Canada. Printed on paper with minimum 30% recycled fibre.
Trafford's print shop runs on "green energy" from solar, wind and other environmentally-friendly power
sources.

Offices in Canada, USA, Ireland and UK

Book sales for North America and international:
Trafford Publishing, 6E–2333 Government St.,
Victoria, BC V8T 4P4 CANADA
phone 250 383 6864 (toll-free 1 888 232 4444)
fax 250 383 6804; email to orders@trafford.com
Book sales in Europe:
Trafford Publishing (UK) Limited, 9 Park End Street, 2nd Floor
Oxford, UK OX1 1HH UNITED KINGDOM
phone +44 (0)1865 722 113 (local rate 0845 230 9601)
facsimile +44 (0)1865 722 868; info.uk@trafford.com
Order online at:
trafford.com/06-2142

10 9 8 7 6 5 4 3

FOREWARD

When I walked hand in hand with my father across a rutted dirt field stubbled with cornstalks to see the plane "Lindy" had flown across the Atlantic, I had no idea of its historic significance. The year was 1927, the place Sioux City Iowa, and I had no notion of what it meant— that plane. It was enough to stand gaping at it in wonder while the men around me talked of the marvelous accomplishment. I was six years old. I had no real idea of what an ocean was. Mountains to me were "Purple Mountain Majesties" carefully crayoned in that hue on my pictures in school.

On that day, I could not imagine the paths my own life would take over the next eight decades, had no thought for anything beyond the perspiration trickling down my nose and the bologna sandwiches Mother had packed for lunch.

Our lives are marked by our stories that stand like stepping-stones across the stream of life.

These are my stories. This is my life.

DEDICATION

To my parents, Paul and Katherine Sturges,
Who taught me to laugh, to dance,
And to tell a story.

ACKNOWLEDGEMENTS

E ver since I began writing stories of my life in the 1980's, I have been encouraged and taught by many people, some mindfully, others by their example.

Teachers of course have played a huge role, beginning with Nina Holzer and Mary Jane Moffat, both creative writing instructors at Foothill College. Both they and the students in their classes were unstinting in their positive critiques, helping me to sharpen these stories.

Then, there was Lynn Rogers, who got me going again after a hiatus of several years, and Sheila Dunnock whose approach to thinking about my life stories helped shape this book. I am indebted to each of them.

And the friends who encouraged me! Phyllis Mattson, author of the poignant *War Orphan in San Francisco,* is a long time supporter whose unfailing devotion and enthusiasm stands out, as well as other members of various writing groups. Thank you all.

A new friend, Betty Auchard, the author of the delightful *Dancing in My Nightgown,* recommended me to her writing coach, Bruce McAllister. Bruce has been a true mentor, guiding me wisely in the progress of the book, telling me

---

honestly when it needed work and encouraging me at every step along the way.

To my editor, Bob Levine, I owe many thanks for his ability to spot errors and to sharpen my sometimes too involved sentences.

Bert, too, has been a wonderful source of support. He has gladly read all the manuscripts I've handed him, making cogent suggestions that I've often taken to heart. His painstaking care in working with the photos in the book has been a godsend!

My daughters—Judy, Cathryn and Joan—have enthusiastically read each story I've sent them and son Jim has helped immensely with computer "know how".

I send my love and gratitude to each of you, and to the many others who have helped with their loving support.

Contents

THE EARLY YEARS
SIOUX CITY

FLOOD

A strange sound, like the hooting of an owl, woke me in the middle of that July night in 1932. I lay in bed, listening to the pounding of raindrops on the roof, frightened, yet not knowing why. The sound came again, this time louder, closer to my room, and suddenly I knew it was Mother uttering those whimpering, frightened cries.

"Dedie, get up!" she said urgently. "There's water—lots of water. We have to go!"

Go where I wondered. Why? We'd had rain before, cloudbursts even, in Sioux City, Iowa and never had to go anywhere. What was Mother talking about? And why was I suddenly afraid? I wished Daddy was home, but he was a traveling man and away during the week.

Mother was shaking Sonny's bed now, pulling the covers off him. "Get up. Get dressed!" she commanded both of us. "We have to get out of the house! I looked out the kitchen window and there was just a <u>wall</u> of water, like a wave, coming at me. The basement's full of water and it's starting to come in the living room! "

I got out of bed, wide-awake now, and pulled on my underpants under my nightgown. Mother grabbed three-year-old Bobby from his small bed, slinging his sleepy body over her shoulder like a sack of potatoes, and disappeared, her nightgown billowing behind her as she ran into her bedroom.

"Hurry, Sonny," I said. "We've got to get dressed fast!"

Off came my nightgown; on went an undershirt and pair of coveralls. Shoes and socks—we'd need those, I thought, clumsily tying the shoelaces. I ran into Mother's room and stood, puzzled at the sight of her smoothing silk stockings onto her legs; sliding feet into her good shoes. Bobby, dressed, sat on the bed watching.

"Come, children, it's time," Mother said again in that urgent tone, edged with panic. Still in her nightgown she scooped Bobby from the bed and shooed Sonny and me ahead of her toward the front door.

"See, the water's starting to come through the register, " she said and I saw a thin trickle edging the square register that vented heat from the coal furnace in winter. Mother grabbed my hand. I tugged at Sonny's and we stepped out onto the front porch.

I stood stock still at the sight that met my eyes. Water, dirty muddy water, fast moving water, covered the front lawn, rolled swiftly down the street. Mother pulled my hand with a sharp yank.

"We've got to get across! It's higher on the other side. We'll go toward the Eckmond's house. Come on!" She stepped boldly out onto where the sidewalk usually was. She'll ruin her silk stockings, I thought. Pulling at my younger brother Sonny's hand and holding onto Mother's tightly, I walked into the swirling water. It sloshed against my eleven year old thighs. The water was warm, like the rainstorms we always had in summer when we kids could go outside and run around in our bare feet squishing mud between our toes. I could have gone barefoot, I thought.

We splashed thru the torrent. People, neighbors on the other side were cheering us on. "You'll make it," they cried and held out hands as we got closer. When I felt the first stub of curb on my foot, I turned to look at the expanse we'd crossed and saw an uprooted tree ricocheting down the street. What if we'd been caught in its branches! I could see myself struggling against the tree, being pushed down into the water. I shivered and turned away from the sight. Strong arms pulled me upward to dry ground. We were safe!

I turned to look at the house I'd always lived in. I would never live there again, but I didn't know it then.

MY FIRST HOME

The house I looked back on as I stood on the neighbor's lawn that morning of the flood was the only home I'd ever known. It, and all the events that I remember up until that dreadful night, have stayed in my memory like barnacles clinging tightly to the hull of a ship. I've scraped them off, one by one, in the stories that follow.

Summers on the front porch are what I remember best about our house in Sioux City. Warm afternoons, with a slight breeze blowing and the soft rustle of the cottonwood trees, while I turned the pages of a favorite book. *The Bobbsey Twins, Five Little Peppers and How They Grew, Heidi, Girl of the Limberlost.*

I was prone to extreme bouts of hunger while I read: *Tarzan's* story made me long for raw lion meat and my mouth watered when Heidi ate her thick slabs of cheese on a mountain path

On that same porch in the time before memory begins, I had been placed in my carriage to nap as an infant. There, too, was the swing where Mother read me colorfully illustrated Bible stories or selections from *The Blue Fairy* book where I was entranced by the adventures of *Rose White and Rose Red,* suffered along with *Hansel and Gretel* in the clutches of the wicked witch.

2100 Terrace Place—I still remember the address after eighty years. Our home was modest, a one-story bungalow with two bedrooms, one bath, living room, dining room and kitchen. Nowadays we would prize it as a Craftsman style

As was usual in midwestern homes, there was a full basement in which reposed the furnace, the coal bin, Mother's Maytag washing machine and various shelves for storing Dad's tools. Mother's preserved fruits and jams, sealed tightly in Mason jars rested on wooden shelves, ready for winter's demands. Clotheslines were strung a few feet below the ceiling.

A single car garage, facing the street of our corner lot, sat at the rear of the property, under an elm tree, which shaded the large green lawn just out the back door of the house. My father built it himself. That garage, with its dirt floor, was the only building project he ever undertook unless you count the dollhouse he made for me one Christmas to my great delight. Little did I know then the significance that garage would have later in my life.

Mother and Dad's bedroom, with the high mahogany bed, matching triple-mirrored dressing table and chest of drawers my mother kept all her life, was a special place to me. It was the bed where I snuggled with her to be comforted, or used as a vantage point, lying on its smooth surface, to watch her sitting at her dressing table, while she brushed and combed her long dark hair and arranged it neatly coiled over her ears in the fashion of the day.

"That looks pretty, mama. It looks like the picture in the magazine."

I'd been looking at photos of the new flapper styles. Mother smiled, putting in another hairpin.

It was in that bed too that I curled up eagerly beside Grandma Sims when she came from her home in Denison, Iowa, to visit. I loved the stories she told me about her childhood in Rockford, Illinois.

"Oh, how I used to love to skate on the Rock River when I was young," she told me, one hand making a swooping movement above my head. "One winter I had a red hat and a scarf so long it almost reached my knees. My brothers didn't have any trouble finding me in that red hat! I skated so fast, sometimes I got ahead of them, and teased them. I had long braids, and they almost stood out straight behind me, I went so fast." I quivered with excitement picturing the scene.

There was a day when I tiptoed into my parents' bedroom. My father had been sick with a fever and in bed for a week. He was sitting on the edge of the bed, pale and thin, and when he smiled at me it was with his mouth closed, not the grin I was used to. Frightened by seeing him so changed, I turned and left the room.

"What's the matter with Daddy?" I asked

"Pyorrhea", Mother said and I didn't ask more. I knew that was something serious and it wasn't long after that my father went to the dentist and came home with bare gums, his face strangely shrunken. I became used to his new false teeth, which he got a few weeks later, and he began to look like my real daddy again. Those teeth never did fit well and from then on he always cut the corn off the cob in the summertime before he could eat it, making little clicking sounds as he chewed.

When I got measles in fourth grade, I was allowed the cool comfort of lying in the big bed with the shades drawn to protect my eyes. Later, bored and healing, climbing out of bed and skittering surreptitiously around on the polished hardwood floor, using the braided rug, like a frog on ice, until I tired and climbed back to the protection of the bed.

"Dedie," mother, suspicious, would call through the door, "are you in bed? You're supposed to be resting, you know." Dedie was the nickname my father had given me as a baby. Juliana was too formal a name for a tiny baby, he thought.

My brother, Sonny, and I shared a bedroom. It was small, with two single beds flanking each wall. When my younger brother Bob was born, his crib was tucked in near the window, at the far side of the room.

I don't have as many memories attached to that room. My own bed, with its pale yellow bedspread, holds most of them: the dreams I sometimes had of a dark amorphous cloud descending on me, which I was powerless to deflect, even by pulling up covers over my head. Or the night I lay awake all the hours till dawn, terrified of the cats howling outside my window.

Our living room was small and cozy with wicker furniture and a flowered carpet in its center. A Bremmer Tully radio was in one corner, where my two years younger brother, Sonny, and I lying on the floor listened to *RinTinTin* or *Little Orphan Annie* while Mother made supper in the kitchen. Or we might be stretched out reading the Sunday funnies, or I, in awe, watching Sonny copy a Norman Rockwell cover of the *Saturday Evening Post*, a stubby pencil in his fingers.

"I'll bet you'll be an artist when you grow up," I'd say, to which he would shake his head. "No way. It's too hard."

In later life, Sonny, now Paul, became a CPA, working and living in many different parts of the world. My younger brother Bob, a lawyer, frequently draws cartoons for the *Law Review* and I paint watercolor scenes when I can find the time. So much for early predictions.

The dining room was graced with Mother's prized dining room set: a polished dark walnut oval table with six matching chairs and a buffet in which she kept her silver and "good" china. I don't remember eating at that table often when I was young except perhaps when Dad was home on the weekends. Once I was absolutely certain I saw the Easter bunny leap quickly from it when I surprised him one dark Easter eve on a return trip from the bathroom.

It was under that table, playing quietly with my doll, that I first heard an argument between my parents. Dad was painting the dining room walls and ceiling that day. The splash of paint in the bucket; the smooth pull of bristles on the ceiling and an occasional *plop* as paint dripped onto the newspaper-lined floor, was strangely comforting. Mother and Dad were talking

"He don't never..." Dad said and Mother interrupted in a low voice. I was sorry for I thought Dad was going to tell her a story. I loved his stories of events and people he met in his work, traveling for Sturges Brothers during the week.

There was silence from Dad instead. Then, in a kind of strangled voice he said,

"If you keep on correcting my grammar, it'll stop me from telling you things."

I sat very still, my heart pounding.

Mother said something softly and went into the kitchen. Pretty soon the painting noise began again, but talking had stopped, and when Dad went out for more paint, I crawled out from under the table, and tiptoed into my bedroom.

Mother must have paid attention to what Dad said, because he didn't stop telling us stories, and I could often hear them talking way into the night.

The kitchen was where I sat with my brothers and waited for hot oatmeal in the morning, or peanut butter and jelly sandwiches at lunchtime. It was where I learned to set the table properly, where Mother showed us the picture book of etiquette she'd bought, pictures that clearly showed the dangers of leaving a spoon in a cup or a glass set too close to the edge of the table. I shuddered inwardly every time I saw that hot cup of cocoa in such danger of being spilled and slapped Sonny's hand when he shoved his glass of milk too close to the edge of the table.

Mother often mopped the linoleum floor in the kitchen, especially after the iceman delivered the fifty pound chunk he put in the icebox in the corner, tracking in through the back door: snow in winter, drips in summer. Sometimes Mother said things under her breath when she mopped,

"Wish he'd..." or "Hope the milk..."

I miss the pink peonies in our back yard. On Monday mornings when Dad carried up the heavy wicker basket of wet clothing from the basement, and I was allowed to spread flat things on the grass, I often carefully draped a white dishtowel over the pink blossoms. They look like mounds of snow now, I would think, longing for winter in the midst of summer in the way of children.

Those were the magic days of childhood when mysteries presented themselves and joys were intensely savored; where comfort came in the circle of loving arms and love showed itself with such subtlety it had no name.

Dancing Mama

Mama used to dance with me when I was a baby. I remember a picture of me, round face peering solemnly over her shoulder, while her right hand held the long skirt off the floor. Was she dancing in the silver pumps with the pointed toes and scoop-backed heels that were part of her wedding outfit the summer before when she married my father? I still have the snapshot of them taken shortly before their wedding. Daddy is looking fondly down at Mama, a slight smile on his face, while she gazes up at him, grinning broadly. It was a life pose for them: Daddy teasing Mama gently and her dismissing laughter, "Oh, Paul"

I heard about dancing from Mama from the time I was old enough to remember. Not ballet or tap, but the kind you did with a partner to soft music—foxtrot or waltz, mostly. There was a new one called the Charleston, and once Mama showed me how she could do that, switching her hands rapidly from knee to knee and kicking her feet in rapid succession. I tried to copy her and ended up on the floor, completely undone by the intricacies of the steps.

When Mama held me on her lap with my head cushioned on her soft bosom to read me a Bible story or an Uncle Wiggly adventure, she used her regular voice, but when she read about Cinderella, her voice took on a special lilt, as if it were her own story.

"...Cinderella was the most beautiful maiden at the ball. Her dress floated behind her in a cloud of pink ruffles. Everyone looked at her as she waltzed with the handsome young prince, who gazed at her adoringly."

I pictured the gleaming floor; a dress with rows and rows of ruffles.

"Can I have a dress with ruffles when I grow up?"

"Of course you can. All the ruffles you want."

The summer I was seven, Mama was pregnant. My younger brother Sonny was always around to play with, but sometimes when he was taking his nap, Mama and I sat in the wood-slat swing on the front porch. Often I would be wearing a thin cotton slip, she a cool nighty to cope with the hot Iowa summer temperatures. We spent a lot of time together. Daddy was a traveling man, gone from Monday till Friday every week. She let me feel her stomach when the baby inside her moved, and sometimes I laid my head on her swollen belly while we swung.

"Do you think it's a girl?" I thought a girl baby would be fun to dress up like I did with my dolls.

"Well, sisters are nice, but sometimes they're mean to you. Brothers tease, but a brother can take you dancing when you grow up." Mama knew what she was talking about because she had two sisters and two brothers.

That settled it. I wanted another brother, added insurance for my adult life. The fact that he would be seven years younger than I when I was in my dancing prime never entered my mind. Besides, I was used to Sonny and the games we played together: climbing trees, roller-skating, roasting filched potatoes over a secret fire in the vacant lot. Sonny would do anything I told him to. Probably another brother would also. A sister was an unknown quantity. A brother would be my first choice.

When Bob was born in September, he was just as I expected, blue-eyed and pink-cheeked, as much like my dolly as a baby girl would have been. I loved him unreservedly. His future potential dissolved in present delight in his round-faced sunny self. I hugged and cuddled him and bragged about him to my friends. The displaced Susanna doll sprawled limply in the corner of my room while I wheeled Bobby up and down the street in her wicker buggy. I taught him to play patty cake and to blow spit bubbles. He was superior to any doll I'd ever had.

Mama and Daddy never went dancing, but sometimes when Daddy was teaching me "K-K-Katie", he would take my hands and dance me around while he sang lustily,

"K-K-Katie, beautiful Katie…
You're the only one that I adore
When the m-moon shines
Over the cowshed;
I'll be waiting for you at the k-k-kitchen door." At which I would burst out giggling at the image of anyone lolling about in the moonlight.

One day while Mama pinned up the hem of a new school dress she'd made for me, she observed my straight ahead feet on the kitchen table where I stood as quietly as I could.

"Point your toes out just a little, Dedie," she said.

"That's the way dancers do. It's more graceful."

"When will I learn to dance, Mama?"

"One of these days I'll teach you. It's a little too soon to start now."

"Does Daddy like to dance?"

"Yes, but not as much as I do. Oh, I was the best dancer on the floor when I was in college!"

"But didn't he have to know how to dance to get into college? Everybody does, don't they?"

"Oh no, honey. Where did you get that idea? But it does make school a lot more fun. Daddy was at a different university, in Nebraska. I guess they danced there too. I didn't know him then. Besides, your father has other qualities..."

I thought about the other qualities: the way Daddy hugged me when he came home on Fridays, calling me his Dedie girl, the times he took me to the circus, just the two of us. Sometimes he brought a present when he came home on Friday night, the funny stories he always had to tell us. I often heard Mama and Daddy's soft laughter way into the night on weekends.

As I grew older, sometime between my eighth and tenth years, Mama began to tell me more about her college days, maybe because she was lonely with Daddy away so much. In any case, she began to talk to me about Mitch, a former beau from those student days.

"Oh, Dedie," she would say, "he was so handsome. And a wonderful dancer. Sometimes I just knew we were the best-looking couple on the floor. When Mitch came to call, all the girls in the sorority were jealous. Sometimes he would take me out in a canoe on the Iowa river..."

Her voice faded and a faraway look came into her eyes. I sat quietly waiting to hear more. "Was he in love with you, Mama?"

"Oh yes. He was such a peach."

"Why didn't you marry him?"

"I think I would have, if he'd asked me. He was a pre-med student. He was studying to be a Psychiatrist, though I never could understand why you'd want to listen to people talk about their problems all day long. But that was what he wanted. And then the war came along and he got a commission. We wrote for awhile, then I didn't hear from him any more."

"Was he hurt in the war?" I didn't want to ask if he'd been killed.

"Yes, he was wounded in France and he married a nurse there. They live in Seattle now. Someone told me he had a very successful practice, as a Psychiatrist."

Then Mama would switch to another topic or tell me abut some of her other beaux.

"I had dates all the time. Sometimes three or four in a day. Oh, it was a grand time…"

Mama had been a Home Economics teacher in the small town of Logan, Iowa before she married Daddy. She spent nine years teaching young girls how to cook and sew. She lived in various townspeople's homes as a boarder during the school year. I think the girls must have loved her with her sparkly eyes and easy laughter. She told me about her teaching days in the small town.

"Sometimes I thought I'd never get married. When you're out of college, there aren't so many available men around. That was all I ever really wanted—to get married and have my own family."

She didn't have to tell me that I was a wanted child, or that she loved my father. I knew it by the way she quoted him and told me what a good man he was. It was only occasionally that she talked about Mitch, but often enough that I remembered. I think he became a preadolescent fantasy lover for me as well. I pictured him as darkly handsome, like Ramon Navarro in the movies.

One summer Monday afternoon, while Mama and I folded clothes, freshly unpinned from the clothesline and still warm from the sun, we heard the thud of the daily paper on the front porch. The *Sioux City Journal's* afternoon delivery was a signal to stop work for a quick scanning of the day's news.

"I'll get the paper, Dedie. You can read the funnies when you finish folding."

Mama didn't come back to the kitchen for a long time. When I went into the living room, the paper lay on the floor in front of her chair. She was sitting there, gazing out the window. I looked at the black headline staring at me from the front page.

SEATTLE DOCTOR SHOT BY IRATE PATIENT, it said.

"It's Mitch," Mama said. "One of his crazy patients broke into his office with a gun and killed him."

She looked so sad that, big as I was then, I curled up on Mama's lap and laid my head on her breast. She held me tight and we sat silent for a long time. At first all I could think of was how glad I was she'd married Daddy instead of Mitch. Then I wondered if Mama would ever teach me to dance, but that didn't seem very important just then.

Traveling Man

M y father was a "traveling man". In the vernacular of the early 1920's, those words described his vocation as a salesman who went "on the road" every week to sell leather goods—harnesses, saddles, bridles, buggy whips—to dealers in the multitude of small towns in Iowa and Nebraska. Those were two of the breadbasket states of the Midwest, famous for tall corn, wheat, alfalfa and livestock.

Dad's old black grip was the silent monitor of his comings and goings: on Monday mornings when he loaded it into the Willys or on Friday night when he set it down inside the kitchen door with a soft thump after a week on the road. Leather, with a pebbly surface, it had started off black, but where it got worn the color turned to brown. Straps encircled it to hold the contents firmly in place.

By Saturday morning, the suitcase would be gone, moved into his and Mother's bedroom to be emptied of its white shirts, dark socks, B-V-D's (the baggy one piece underwear he always wore) and the ties for when he was calling on customers. I think of the good leather smell of that bag, a smell reminiscent of the leather factory owned by my grandfather Ernest and his brother, Uncle Charlie. "Sturges Brothers Harness and Saddlery" the sign above the door read, and the two men, smoking their cigars in the small office, each with his own desk and spittoon, were as familiar a sight to me as the life-sized model horse outside the door wearing its fancy collar and saddle. My father was their salesman. As the eldest son who was expected to someday take over the business, it was a natural place for him to fit in.

"Want to go down to the shop, Dedie?" Dad would sometimes ask me on a Saturday morning. He'd given me the nickname Dedie. I think Juliana was just too formal a name for him to call a tiny baby.

I loved going with him, sitting importantly beside him on the leather seat of the Model T Ford he drove. Uncle Charlie and Grandpa would be sitting, heads wreathed in blue cigar smoke. I would greet them briefly before I could run and play in the huge warehouse of supplies: shiny saddles, hanging in rows above bins of straps, hardware, buggy whips. I loved to get into one of the wheeled carts that transported goods from one area of the warehouse to another and laughed aloud when one of the workers pushed me rapidly from aisle to aisle. Above all, I savored the smell of pungent leather, saddle soap, and wax.

Sometimes I try to imagine what life was like for Dad, away from his family so much. I can picture him settling into the car on a Monday morning, the back seat loaded with samples: buggy whips, blinders, harness, maybe some hardware for use with the multitude of straps that bind a horse. He never got a very early start on Mondays because he always helped Mother with the washing before he left home. I was accustomed to seeing my father, cigar smoke drifting upward as he held the strong smelling yellow Fels Naptha laundry soap against the curve of his belly, cutting it expertly into narrow strips that *plopped* one at a time into the churning hot water of the washing machine. He would grunt a little as he pulled heavy sheets or towels through the wringer into the blue rinse water and exhale softly after lugging the heaped wicker basket full of wet laundry up the steep stairs to the backyard where Mother and I hung it out in the sunshine.

Then it was time to leave and he did so quickly, pulling his hat forward to shield his blue eyes and swinging his legs under the steering wheel with an ease born of long practice. "See you Friday," he'd say to Mother, giving her a pecking kiss and starting the engine.

But once Dad was "on the road", I think he probably set his mind on the week ahead, the customers he would see, the roads he would travel to encompass his territory for the week. I can imagine him stepping into a harness shop, greeting the owner by name.

"Fred," he'd say. "How's it going?"

"Well, Paul. Glad to see you. Say, I heard that fellow over in Remson had a little trouble last week. Is he o.k?"

"Yeah, he's fine. It was a funny thing though, the trouble he got into. It seems his dog...." and Dad would chuckle a little, push his hat brim off his forehead, and be off on one of his famous stories that assured his welcome wherever he went. There was never a bite of meanness in his telling and he was as apt to relate a story where he was the butt of a joke as he was to recount the embarrassment of another.

"Say, Paul, why don't you drop by for supper? The wife's fixing some chicken—we've got plenty."

And Dad would go to his hotel room, take a clean shirt out of his grip and write up his orders for the day before going to his customer's house.

I'm sure though, that there were many nights when he sat alone in his room, after a solitary meal at some diner. Meat and potatoes, maybe some pie (though Mother made it better than anyone else) a cup of coffee. Mother always said Dad was a "meat and potatoes" man, which no doubt accounted for his comfortable girth, and probably contributed to his high blood pressure in later years. Some nights I know he sat at his typewriter, another piece of luggage that always went into the car on Mondays. I can see him, a green eyeshade to protect from the glare of the overhead light in the barely furnished room, pecking away at the keys. Sometimes he would laugh aloud while he wrote his monthly column "Horse Sense and Nonsense" for the *Harness World*, a trade magazine as familiar to me as the *Saturday Evening Post*.

I think about the extremes of Iowa weather and I can picture him enduring it. Putting chains on the tires in the heavy Iowa snowstorms, his fingers blue with cold, his breath fuming around his head. I can see him staring straight ahead, straining to see in the heavy downpour of a summer cloudburst, cursing softly to himself as he hears the familiar *thump thump* of a flat tire. I have to imagine the language: I never heard my father swear.

Those early cars had no heaters: Air-conditioning is a recent development. I can imagine the gloved hands, the heavy overcoat, and earmuffs on a below-zero day, to say nothing of the hot water for the windshield, the long warm-up for the engine. In summer there must have been sweat dripping into his eyes on a blistering hot day, perhaps a wet washcloth on the back of his neck.

And all the time, my Dad was thinking. Making up stories, polishing ones he'd heard from his last customer to make a better version for the next one. Thinking about us at home, what he'd bring Mother, how he'd hug my brothers and me. One time Mother said to me,

"You know, your father said to me once, 'I get scared when I'm almost home on Fridays, afraid I'll hug the kids too hard and hurt them.' He was crazy about you children."

Mother would tell me things like that because Dad was not demonstrative, at least not that I can remember. I don't recall sitting on his lap, or being held in his arms, and was envious of a cousin whose father jiggled her on his knee while he talked. But Uncle Alan couldn't tell stories like my Dad; couldn't make Friday the best day of the week just because he came home and set down that piece of worn luggage—his grip—just inside the door.

Sandbox Politics

The rug on the living room floor scratches my bare legs as I sit waiting for my father to finish reading his newspaper. My left shoulder leans against his right leg; his black polished shoe reflects light from the window. I can smell the polish. Cigar smoke curls about the room making trailing patterns to the open door. The paper crackles with the turning pages.

I am content to wait. Daddy has promised to take me with him to "The Shop" after he finishes reading. I love to go there with him. He lets me play in the warehouse when he talks to Grandpa and Uncle Charley. I love the leathery smell of the place.

Daddy has never told me to be quiet, not to disturb, yet I know that is part of the bargain we have struck. We often do things quietly together. When we go somewhere by car, he puts me in the front seat and slams the door so the lock is in place, then walks around to his side and slams his door too. The slippery leather upholstery makes me slide down toward the floor and I hitch back in the seat. All of the inside of our box-like Ford of the nineteen twenties is black, except for the shiny brown wood on the instrument panel, which is about all I can see except for sky and the tops of trees.

Daddy drives staring straight ahead with a *thinking* look on his face and I watch out of the corner of my eye to see when it is o.k. to start talking. When I do, telling him about school or whatever I talk to my father about, his usual response is a grunt. "Hmph." I know that is because he is driving and must concentrate and not to be taken as a sign of displeasure. All the same, I'm careful to say what I think he wants to hear. Daddy likes stories about things that happen to me. Today I tell him about an incident during the week when he was away working.

"Sonny followed me to the Hayses' the other day when I went over to play in their back yard. I was going across the bars and Mrs. Hayes came out and said I had to take him home. I said why? And she said Sonny threw sand in Janie's eyes and we couldn't play there anymore. Not ever again, she said."

"Hmph. Then what?"

"Then we went home. We both felt bad. Sonny said Leo threw sand at him first and then Janie got in the way, But Mrs. Hayes probably wouldn't believe him if he told her. It wasn't fair because Sonny didn't mean to hurt Janie and I didn't do anything but she kicked me out too."

"Well, you've got a swing in the backyard. And a sandbox."

"I know. But they've got more stuff and all the kids go there to play. I don't like Janie and Leo much—they think they're smart because they've got rings and a slide too. Sonny and I didn't have anyone to play with."

"Humph. What'd you do?"

"I made Sonny apologize. He didn't want to. But I said we couldn't play over there unless he did and I'd go with him because he's scared of Mrs. Hayes. I am too. I had to talk to him a lot, but then we went and I rang the doorbell."

"Humph?"

"She looked really cross and scary when she opened that Dutch door of theirs and looked down at us. But I said Sonny came to say he was sorry and wouldn't throw sand and could we please play? She looked at Sonny hard and said Is that right? And he said yes, so she said well all right—go ahead, but BEHAVE yourself!"

"Pretty good. You bearded the lion in her den."

I didn't know what that meant, but I could tell by the little smile on Daddy's face that he thought I'd figured things out pretty well.

The story I didn't tell my father about that week was one only Sonny and I knew. I still shuddered a little when I remembered that day when we built the fire in the vacant lot across the street, the one that was full of dry grass this time of year.

My brother and I loved to go there, sometimes with a neighbor boy, sometimes just the two of us. We had dug out a little hollow of dirt, just the right size for a small fire made from twigs and grass. I was the oldest, at seven, the ringleader, the one to stealthily grab a handful of wooden kitchen matches when Mother's back was turned; or quietly tiptoe down the basement stairs to sneak potatoes from their sack and hastily stuff them into my pockets for later roasting. I enjoyed the feeling of guilt and daring as I raced back across the street after one of these forays. Anyway,

Mother was too busy with our new baby brother, Bobby, to pay much attention to us.

On the day I was remembering, Sonny and I had sat quietly smoking hollow weeds, waiting for the potatoes to cook. There was a gentle breeze, and the warm sun made me sleepy. Suddenly Sonny jumped up and tugged at my sleeve,

"Dedie, look! The fire, it's spreading!"

I saw the little patches of blackened grass, tendrils of flame getting bigger as I watched.

"Stamp on it, Sonny, squash it out!"

I jumped up, started stomping as fast as I could, panic licking in my breast. What had I done? The fire seemed to be spreading in many directions. Sonny and I stomped frantically, silently, breathing hard. Finally, the flames were gone and only blackened weeds remained. Potatoes forgotten, we raced across the street to the safety of our home.

Maybe I would tell Daddy another time, maybe not.

GRANDMA'S HOUSE

I had two sets of grandparents. My mother's parents, Jacob and Anna Sims, lived in Denison, a town sixty some miles south of Sioux City. My father's parents, Ernest and Nell Sturges, lived in Sioux City and many Sundays were spent with them when our family gathered in their home after church for Sunday dinner. Sometimes my father's brothers, George and Ernest and their families would be there too.

Grandma Sturges' house comes back to me in pleasurable sensations: a place of sunshine, anticipatory odors, laughter and longings never voiced.

I click up the stairs in my Sunday shoes pausing to look out the rose-colored stained glass window, which spills warm light where the steps turn. The large elm tree outside looks strangely black; the sky behind it lavender. How can a pink glass do that, I wonder. . Still loving the sound of my new shoes on the hard wood, I reach the second floor and hear what I had expected: the ticking of many clocks, like cicadas on a warm summer night. They line the wall outside of Grandma's bedroom. Grandpa likes to collect them and sometimes I wonder how he can sleep with so many clocks ticking and chiming.

I am in the big double bed with its feather pillows and the comforter that Grandma has made. I have been in that bed for two weeks because I have bronchial pneumonia and Grandma has offered to care for me while I convalesce. Smiling broadly at me, she brings me hot soup, bread and milk on a tray. The thick lenses on her spectacles make her blue eyes look wet and shiny.

"Eat your soup," she says. "Dr. Klingan is going to come and visit you this afternoon."

The doctor will listen to my chest after he pops a thermometer in my mouth. I hope he says that I must stay in bed another week. I love being here in this cocoon of a bed. It is fun to be sick and pampered. I am five years old. I don't know it now, but I will never again have pneumonia.

My stomach gurgles, and I barely hear the pleasant hum of conversation, low laughter and the sound of silverware clicking on plates as I sit at the long dining room table, surrounded by aunts and uncles and cousins. There is a platter of fried chicken on the table, serving dishes piled with mashed potatoes, green beans, a gravy boat brimming with brown gravy. The smell of chicken overwhelms the rest and I hope Grandpa will give a short blessing so I can begin to eat. Breakfast was a long time ago, before Sunday school and church. My stomach gurgles again. Cousin Mary Marie nudges me with her elbow and whispers

"You want to play hide and seek after dinner?" We giggle

I am in the claw-footed bathtub in the upstairs bathroom, soaking in warm water and lazily soaping myself. I am eleven years old, and our family is staying at Grandma's because our house has been flooded and the basement is full of water. I discover one long hair in my pubic region and think it is a strange place for a hair to be. When I tell Mother, who is also in the room, she looks funny but says it is nothing to worry about—it's part of growing up.

On that same summer, I have been sleeping out in the glassed in sleeping porch just off the bedroom I was in when I was sick. My brothers each have a bed on the porch too and sometimes we sneak down the back stairs to the kitchen at night to see if we can find cookies to eat.

Daddy has told us the story about what happened when he and his brothers slept on the same porch and one night were making too much noise and jumping on the beds. Grandpa got mad, and yelled at the boys to be quiet. When they didn't, he stuck his head through the window separating his bedroom from the porch—except he didn't notice the window was closed and banged it so hard with his head he cracked the glass with his forehead and made it bleed.

"We got quiet after that," daddy said.

My brothers and I are careful to keep the noise level down, even though it's only our parents sleeping there now.

Grandma and I are going to make a pumpkin pie. We go into her pantry and the smell of spices—cinnamon, allspice, and ginger—makes me sniff appreciatively. Grandma is wearing a long apron over her housedress and her glasses slide down a little on her nose. She tips the metal lined flour bin out and scoops a generous amount into a mixing bowl. "You get the cinnamon and ginger and cloves," she says, "Oh and that milk on the counter—I'll bring the eggs and lard and sugar."

Hands full, we make our way to the kitchen table. "You can mix the milk and eggs and pumpkin in this bowl," she says, as I stir with the big wooden spoon. "Now we'll put the spices in," and I watch as she measures them carefully into the bowl.

"I'll do the rest—you were a good help. You can go and read now."

I walk through the dining room into the darker living room with its bay window and the big Chesterfield sofa I love to curl up in to read. There are pillows of all kinds and shapes and colors on the sofa and I rearrange a tasseled one to fit my head. The mohair of the cushions scratches my bare legs and I scrunch them up to avoid as much contact with skin as possible. I've already selected my favorite book to read from the glass-fronted bookcase, Ernest Thompson Seton's *Wild Animals I Have Known*, and I begin to relive the adventures of Lobo the Wolf. The beaded fringe of the silk lampshade tinkles as I reach up to turn on the light, and I glance up at the oval picture with its polished mahogany frame of my long-dead Aunt Julia from whom part of my name comes. It's hard to think of the auburn-haired, rosy-cheeked twelve-year-old girl in the picture as my aunt, for she died of diphtheria so long ago.

"I reached in and tried to pull the phlegm out of her throat, but nothing helped." Grandma has told me. "Oh, I wish…but I'm so glad we had that picture made just before she got sick. So many died…"

Pumpkin pie fragrances drift in from the kitchen. I snuggle deeper into the cushions and lose myself in the story.

LESSONS LEARNED

When I set off in September of 1926, skipping happily along with a few neighborhood friends, to attend my first day of Kindergarten, I had no idea of the lessons the next few hours would teach me. I don't know why my mother didn't accompany me to school that first day, as I always did with my own children.

Perhaps customs were different then; perhaps she remained at home to take care of my younger brother, Sonny. Dad would not have been available since he left for his weekly trip "on the road" on Monday mornings.

In any case, I was looking forward eagerly to Kindergarten. Mother had walked me to Hunt School during the summer. I roller-skated beside her as we traversed the blocks of the mile that separated our house from the school and found that day a method for stopping suddenly when nothing else worked: just sit down on the sidewalk! I didn't know it then, but I would roller-skate to school many times in the next few years, often leaving bits of skin on Sioux City's walkways when I fell. I recall little else about that introduction to the school's location, but I was certain I knew the way perfectly.

In fact, as our small group walked together on that first day, I was studying the blocks; where the turns were and the location of the tree-lined streets we traversed as we walked. It was as I remembered and I was sure I could find my way home at noontime, when my school day would be over. All the other kids were in more advanced grades and would be coming home later in the day.

I remember the class full of wriggling children, all strangers but one, my friend Priscilla. Priscilla was a very self contained child who lived in another part of town and whose father was a banker who had once confused me greatly when he asked me in a solemn voice,

"Hello, Juliana. And how many years have you seen?"

Seen? How did one see a year? A five year old has not that many years to consider. I stammered embarrassingly, blushing, when he amended his statement, "And how old are you?" a question I could answer.

Anyway, Pris was the spur for my first real lesson that day. In my eagerness to greet her, to tell her something funny, I forgot the teacher's firm instructions, given in a no-nonsense voice that her pupils were not to engage in conversation without permission. Clasping my hand over my mouth to keep my excited giggles from erupting, I heard my name called,

"Juliana, don't you remember what I just said?"

I looked around in bewilderment, for of course I didn't.

"You did not have permission to be talking with Priscilla, did you?'

I shook my head "no".

"Then you will need to spend the next five minutes

over in the corner where there is no one to talk with. Please face the wall so you won't see anyone either."

Doing as I was told, I spent a long five minutes listening to the other sounds of the classroom before I returned to my seat, not particularly chastened and ready to join in whatever fun was at hand. I do recall the incident, but not with any feeling of trauma. It made me more careful of when I talked, but certainly didn't affect my verbalization on any subject, especially what I perceived to be funny ones.

There were other learning experiences that morning too. Certainly raising my hand to ask permission was one; perhaps coloring in the lines of an art book another. At the end of the morning, which came at about eleven thirty, I was eager for the next phase of my day: walking home alone to have lunch with Mother and Sonny and tell them about my morning.

When the dismissing bell rang, I walked confidently out the school's front door and headed for home. I was about to have another new experience.

My memory of the next half hour is very clear: I see myself walking the long sidewalk from the school to the street, waving goodbye to new friends; see myself turn right onto the main street and walk confidently in a route I was sure was correct, block after block, waiting for familiar houses to appear. I can see the dappled shade on the hot cement, feel the perspiration on my forehead, taste the dryness of my mouth. But where was the house where the Pekinese dogs that always barked at me lived in? Where were the steep steps that led up to my friend Mary's house? Why did things look so different on this wide avenue?

I began to cry. Gone was the happy anticipation of Mother's smiling face, of the peanut butter sandwich and milk for lunch. Instead, I suddenly realized, I was lost. The tears were falling faster now; I licked them away with my tongue, swiped them with my wrist.

Ahead of me, on the corner, a Model T Ford sat with its engine idling, a man at the wheel. A man with a hat like daddy wore. He leaned out the window, and said,

"Hello, little girl. Are you lost?"

"I think so," I blubbered.

"Well, maybe I could help you. I'm waiting to pick up my son in the school over there." He pointed to a school across the street that I hadn't noticed, or ever seen before.

"I—I'm lost," I said. "But if you could take me to the Piggly Wiggly store, I know my way home from there!"

"Well, hop in. I know where that store is." He reached across the front seat to open the car door.

An immense relief swept over me. He could help! Not once did I think of the warnings Mother had given me about strange men in cars; never considered that I might be in for trouble. Heaving myself onto the running board, and then onto the black leather seat of the Model T (just like daddy's!) I said again,

"I can find my way home from the Piggly Wiggly store."

True to his word, the driver made straight for the store and I was again on familiar turf.

"Turn at the next corner," I said, "then go a bunch of blocks. I'll tell you when to turn again." And soon, "There's my house! And my mother out in front!"

I wondered why Mother's smile looked so blurry; why

she thanked the stranger so many times, but I was in too much of a hurry for that peanut butter sandwich to spend time listening to grownups. I headed for the house. I was home and hungry and safe.

ooooo

The lessons learned from that experience were, at the time, subliminal, but as I think back I know attitudes were formed: I could trust some strangers, I could find my way if I had the right starting point. And I wasn't always going in the right direction.

That self confident, sometimes mistaken little girl resides in me still. I know it when I take off for a solitary walk in a strange city. Though now I am very careful to mark landmarks as I go, exhilaration possesses me and I walk on filled with energy, discovering new sights and sounds as though they had been freshly created just for me, just for this moment. I felt it when I climbed the hill behind the Parthenon in Athens, picturing the ancient shoppers in the Plata, and stumbling on the marble steps. I was captured by the same sense of adventure one warm October late afternoon in Boston, when I decided to walk the Freedom Trail unaccompanied.

That particular trip was very reminiscent of my first Kindergarten day for without checking the facts, I assumed the trail would be a circular one, ending where I started on Boston Commons. Not so, I discovered as the dusk fell in a strange neighborhood, which my imagination told me was full of gangsters and other nefarious types. There was no friendly stranger to rescue me that time, and I ended my walk by calling a taxi from a hole-in-the-wall bar's payphone to take me safely back to my hotel room.

Most of the things I learned in school became part of my consciousness without much volition, like a blotter slowly seeping up spilled water. Cursive writing, reading, multiplication tables were skills that became part of me.

Apparently the teachers were part of this silent seepage as well. Where have all the teachers gone? I don't remember a single one, except as shadowy figures giving directions in the front of the room. I can hear the click of chalk on the blackboard, see the multiplication table written there or an example of good penmanship, but not one teacher's face or name do I recall. I liked school. I was good at it, remembering my times tables and doing careful cursive circles, like perfect Snaky toys.

One clear memory I do have is the introduction to classical music. I can smell the sawdusty, linseed oil odors of that long hall where we children sat on the floor with our backs to the wall, waiting for the voice in the loudspeaker to begin.

"Good morning, boys and girls! This is the Walter Damrosch hour and we are going to listen to a composer named Grieg who wrote *In the Hall of the Mountain King*. I want you to listen for the rushing water sounds as they tumble over the mountain rocks..." Or, another morning, a description of Tchaikovsky's *Swan Lake* ballet. I could picture the swans gliding soundlessly in the cool water. I didn't know then that swans are sometimes vicious birds that bite ferociously when provoked.

Some things I learned vicariously. I never "sassed" a teacher, especially after I saw what talking back could do. I can still hear the angry strides of our third grade teacher as she marched back to Mary Cremmin's desk grabbing her shoulders and shaking them. Back and forth, back and forth Mary's dark hair flew while I watched in fascination. When the teacher went back to her desk, Mary sat at hers with a subdued look on her face, and I turned quickly back to my paper and the penmanship exercise that the class had been practicing. What Mary said to provoke such action I never knew, but Mary had inspired awe in me by her stoic endurance of humiliation. How embarrassed and afraid I would be if a teacher got really angry with me! My stomach grew tight just thinking of it.

That night, in the diary my father had given me, I drew a stick figure picture of Mary's flying curls, the teacher standing above her grabbing her shoulders. Sometimes it helped to laugh at things you were afraid of. When I showed it to Daddy on the weekend, we laughed together at the picture and I felt better.

The lessons I learned outside of the schoolroom were important too.

When my little brother, Bobby was born in September of 1928, I was sure he was the cutest, smartest baby ever born, with the bluest eyes and most engaging grin in the world. And I was not one to keep that knowledge to myself, so that every day I had a new story to tell: his first laugh, the bubbles he could blow, the rattle he could shake. One day, after a couple of weeks of my chatter, one of my schoolmates said to me,

"Oh for heaven's sake, Juliana, do you think you're the only one who ever had a baby brother at home? We're tired of hearing about him."

If I'd had a tail, I would have slunk away, but instead I stopped telling stories about Bobby. It was a cruel but ultimately valuable lesson: not everyone is interested in all you have to say. Other people have stories too.

There was no cafeteria at our school: we children went home for lunch each day. One morning, though, when the icicles hung long from our roof and the milk bottle top rose two inches above the lip, Mother said to me,

"Dedie, it is just too cold for you to come home for lunch today. I've called Mrs. Pritchard—you remember her. She lives just across the street from the school and she will fix something for you to eat."

At lunchtime, I put on my warm coat and hat, my galoshes and gloves and walked across the street to Mrs. Pritchard's. The two of us sat at her dining room table and I used my best manners, saying please and thank you and feeling very strange and trying to think of things to say, and to answer her questions the best I could. We ate cream of tomato soup with oyster crackers and I can still remember that hard chair and shiny tabletop and the steam rising off the soup.

Going to Mrs. Pritchard's house that noon had felt strange, as though I were entering another, unfamiliar world where I might be gauche and awkward and disgrace myself in some way. But instead I learned about being polite and talking to a strange grownup without the buffeting effect of a parent that day.

When I think back on that first day at school, I marvel at the freedom we children had in those days. Now, a child would never be allowed to walk home alone from kindergarten! I think the confidence I had in the goodness of strangers was reinforced that day, and I am grateful for that. It could have been so different, and might have affected my attitudes about people in later life.

Walking back and forth to school was taken for granted. Now we ferry kids everywhere, and necessarily so, but the exercise my brothers and I got every day was a habit we have all kept in one way or another. Paul, at eighty-two, chafes because he can't quite manage his daily five mile hike and is down to three. Bob keeps in shape from his largely sedentary work as an attorney by swimming, playing racquetball and his New Year's Day annual bike ride to Mt. Hamilton and back. And I still walk or swim or dance each day. We remember the lessons of childhood and they become part of us for a lifetime.

WEE MACGREEGOR
AND OTHER MATTERS

I sit on the wooden swing on the front porch of Grandma Sims' house in Denison. I am visiting my mother's mother for two weeks, the longest time I have been away from home by myself in my life. It is hot on this July day, hot and quiet with only the sound of the flies buzzing outside and Grandma's voice lilting above me. My legs are sticky with perspiration; sweat beads my nose and runs down onto my lips. I move my bottom a little to ease the pressure of the hard wooden slats of the swing, careful not to disturb the magic of the story. Cousin Ann Mary's bare feet stick out on the other side of Grandma, toes wiggling slightly. Neither of us makes a sound, so absorbed are we in the story.

Grandma is reading about "Wee Macgreegor" the little Scotch boy who is proving his bravery at the zoo.

"If a beast wis guan fur to pu'ma heid aff,...I-I-I wud gi'e 't kick!" he says loudly. I hardly notice it is Grandma's voice.

I shiver slightly, knowing Macgreegor is very small. A

kick at a lion would put him in danger. Grandma knows how to speak the Scottish burr perfectly, I think. I could listen forever. I know she will stop at the end of the chapter and I will have to wait until tomorrow to hear another adventure of Wee Macgreegor's. It is no use begging, for grandma always does what she promises, and the promise is one chapter each afternoon while Ann Mary and I are visiting.

We rest every afternoon from one o'clock until three. I am upstairs in the bedroom over the kitchen, wearing only my white cotton slip. The books in the bookcase are thick and leather bound. I read the titles—*Oliver Twist, David Copperfield, a Tale of Two Cities*. Nothing here to interest my eleven-year-old self. I wish for one of my *Tarzan* books or one of the Guy de Maupasant stories from the bookcase downstairs, but I shouldn't go there until three o'clock. I tiptoe into the little bedroom at the end of the hall, and drop to my knees onto the wooden floor. My chin rests in my hands, elbows on the low windowsill. I stare straight across at the interior of the room in the house next door. The curtains are drawn back, to invite cool breezes. The scene is laid before me like a painting. There is a high bed like the one Mother was in when Bobby was born and we went to the hospital to see our new baby brother. On the bed is a thin young woman whose face juts ceiling-ward, sharp and motionless. Today the face is very pale, but when I look into the room at night, the light gives the skin a greenish pallor.

I know who the young woman is. Her name is Maxine Robinson. She is the only child of the dentist and his wife who live in the big two-story brick house next door. I know

Maxine has a harp, for I saw it one time when Mother and I went to call on the Robinson's. I have heard the sweet rippling music on summer evenings before Maxine got sick. But now Maxine is very ill. Grandma has told me that Maxine went to Europe in the winter to study the harp and came home with a fever and cough that wouldn't go away. She didn't go to see a doctor—

"The Robinson's are Christian Scientists," Grandma told me. "They don't believe in doctors. Now they say she has T.B."

I go back to my bed; lie on the rough cotton coverlet. The vision of her pale face stays with me and I shiver a little, despite the heat.

Ann Mary and I have been playing paper dolls and dress-up all day. We are out on the North porch where it is cooler than anywhere else in the house, except maybe the basement. The North porch is long and narrow, with a row of windows facing the back yard. Today they are all open to catch the breeze. My cousin and I sit on the narrow cot against the wall absorbedly cutting and crayoning the paper creations we have made for our one-dimensional paper dolls. Mine is Janet Gaynor, my favorite movie star, and I have made dresses for her of every style and color I can think of. I draw the tabs carefully, so that the paper clothes will fit, and hum to myself. Occasionally we make comments to one another.

"Look, Dedie, isn't this red dress pretty?" Ann Mary says, showing me her doll.

Or—"Shoes are really hard to cut out—especially heels."

This morning Grandma opened the trunk with all

the old clothes in it. She said some my mother wore when she was young, and some belonged to Ann Mary's daddy, Uncle Alan. There were things of Aunt Marianna and Uncle Jim's and Aunt Marjorie's too. We tried on some of them, but it was too hot to wear them long. I told Grandma I was sweating and she said,

"Juliana, men and horses sweat. Ladies PERSPIRE!" I could tell she meant it too, because her mouth got straight and closed in a straight line when she said that. I remember that Mother has told me how angry Grandma can get, how frightened Mother was of her sometimes. I must remember to perspire.

"Do you miss your mother, Dedie?"

"No, not yet." I have only been visiting here for five days so far. I don't want to ask Ann Mary if she misses her mother because Aunt Patty is dead and I don't want to remind her about that. Of course, Aunt Patty died several years ago and Ann Mary is probably used to it by now. Anyway, Aunt Marjorie always treats Ann Mary a little special and that probably makes up for it.

'Has anyone told you about periods yet?" I ask my cousin. I always tell her the new things Mother tells me, in case her daddy hasn't gotten around to it. Too, it makes me feel superior if I know something she doesn't. I just got this information from Mother last month, a week before my eleventh birthday. Ann Mary is eleven too, a month older than I.

We talk in whispers. I tell her about the little show of blood that comes once and then you know you're a woman and can have babies. We go back to our paper dolls.

Aunt Marjorie and Grandma are sitting at the dining

room table with us. Aunt Marjorie is a Home Ec teacher in Philadelphia and always comes to visit Grandma in the summer. She doesn't have a husband, and Mother says it is probably too late for her to get one. She has brown eyes and wavy brown hair. Her eyes crinkle up at the corners when she laughs and she really listens to you when you tell her things. Grandma says to Aunt Marjorie, "Oh how Papa would have enjoyed..."

They are talking about Grandpa Sims who died last winter when he was eighty years old. That seems very old to me, but Mother said Grandma thought he died too soon. Grandpa is a distant figure to me. He was very dignified and I don't remember playing with him often, but I still have the Bible he gave me on my tenth birthday, inscribed "To Juliana on her tenth birthday from Jacob Sims." I had felt shy about asking him to write in it, but he wrote very carefully and didn't seem to mind.

"There you are, young lady," he said, and gave me a pat on my shoulder before I left the room.

The Kandy Kitchen smells of cool vanilla ice cream, mint candies and chocolate syrup. All its surfaces are hard—the marble counter tops, the round white tables, chairs with butterfly wing shaped wire backs, the glass cases on the counter filled with chocolates and candied almonds; jelly beans and licorice whips. The silver spigots that pour forth chocolate or butterscotch syrups gleam in the sunlight. Grandma sits primly between Ann Mary and me while we pore over the menu. I can imagine all the offerings— chocolate sundaes, banana splits, and strawberry sodas. Finally I decide, as I knew from the start I would, on a butterscotch sundae with nuts and whipped cream. Ann

Mary always gets a chocolate soda and Grandma a dish of vanilla ice cream. We eat in silence, concentrating on the smooth sweetness, turning the glass slowly counterclockwise to spoon out every bit of syrup at the bottom. Ann Mary's straw makes a gurgling sound as she sucks in to get the last bit of chocolate.

"Come girls, it's time to leave," Grandma says and we walk out into the heat of the day. It is slow walking with Grandma and I lessen my pace and think about the movie I have just seen. The beautiful face of the heroine floats before me and I vow to have a long ruffled dress like hers when I grow up.

Grandma points to the two story red brick building on the opposite corner of the street. "Do you see the offices upstairs, girls? Where it says Page & Norelius? Your grandfather was the senior partner in that firm. Mr. Page came as a young lawyer years ago and now he is the senior partner. Mr. Norelius is the junior partner now. Grandpa was a very well respected man in this town. He was a most upright man. You must always remember that you belong to one of the best families in the community." She walked very straight, and I stood as tall as I could beside her.

It is the morning of the last day of my visit. Daddy will come to get me about ten o'clock. I climb out of bed and notice salmon pink stains on my flowered cotton nightie. There is a little on the sheet too. I know what is happening and I tell Grandma. She gives me a clean piece of flannel to pin to my underpants.

Later, I sit on the front seat of the car with my father, chattering to him about my visit. He grunts occasionally, chewing the stub of his cigar as he drives. Sometimes he laughs at one of my stories. He tells me about a few of the people he has seen during his week of travel. Some of the names are familiar and I feel friendly toward the unknown strangers he talks about. Daddy asks me if I was homesick. I tell him no, there was too much to do.

We arrive in Sioux City at noon. As we turn the corner into our familiar street, a lump rises in my throat. I jump from the car, tears welling, and run into the house.

"Mother, Mother, where are you? I missed you so. I'm so glad to be home! Something happened to me this morning..."

I am enfolded in my mother's arms.

Aftermath

This has been the most mixed-up summer of my life, I thought to myself as I fastened the straps of the second hand tap shoes Mother had bought from a friend. I was taking tap dancing lessons at a summer school near Grandma Sturges' house. I didn't know any of the girls in the class and I felt clumsy all the time. That was the way I felt even when I wasn't in class: clumsy and out of place, ever since the flood and not being able to live in my own house, or play with the kids in our neighborhood there. It didn't seem much like a summer vacation, a summer that had started off so well with my visit to Denison and Grandma Sims' house in June.

But that awful flood in July had changed everything. Our whole family had been forced to move in with Daddy's parents, Grandpa and Grandma Sturges, here in Sioux City, and it was August already. Being here had started out sort of like an adventure at first—we kids were used to being at Grandma's house—but now we all wanted to go home. We still couldn't move back there because the water wasn't all pumped out of the basement yet, and there was still a lot of mud in it too.

"It's a mess," I'd heard my father say to Mother. "There's two feet of mud all over the basement floor. The washing machine is ruined; all the jars of fruit you canned are broken. The furnace will need a lot of work. I'll have to hire someone, I guess." His voice sounded tired, not like usual.

And later, after another frustrating weekend, "Got an estimate today from an outfit that can clear out the basement. But it's high—it'll cost $1200.00. Don't know where I'll get the money—have to try to borrow it, I guess."

I knew there was something called a Depression, that lots of men were out of work, that Daddy sometimes said his week on the road hadn't been "very good." I was old enough now, at eleven, to remember a little of the stock market crash of 1929 and the black headlines that went with it. Once when Mother and I were shopping at *Pelletier's* department store downtown, she'd told me that one of the owners had jumped out of a sixth story window because he lost so much money in the crash.

"Did he die?"

"Yes, dear. But his family got some insurance money, I think." I shuddered, imagining him opening the window, standing on the sill and looking down. How scared he must have been.

Now it was 1932 and for several years Grandpa's business had suffered because the farmers didn't have money to buy new leather goods for their horses. The drought just kept going every summer and prices for farm goods had gone way down. Some farmers even poured milk out on the streets rather than sell it for almost nothing.

Mother and Dad and my grandparents often talked in

the evenings around the dining room table. I could hear their low voices, as I read in the adjacent room. One evening I heard part of a conversation.

"You can stay here as long as you like."

"But we're putting you out…"

One night, Mother said quietly, after they'd talked awhile. "My mother's all alone now that Papa's gone. We could live there, just until—"

And Dad said, "Sure hate to leave our own house. But Denison's only sixty miles from here… I could still keep on working the same as I have been."

Then Mother's voice again. "There's the children's school starting next month to think about. And Dedie does need a room of her own now."

"Maybe it's the only way we can manage…" I could hardly hear Dad's voice.

And so it's been decided. We're going to move to Denison and live with my other grandmother, Grandma Sims. She's got plenty of room and she wants us to come. I'll have my own room and won't have to share it with my brothers. I'm exited about moving, but Mother doesn't seem so very happy. I found her wiping away tears the other day.

"Aren't you glad we can go live with Grandma Sims?" I asked. "Why are you crying?"

"I just hate to leave my own house, not be able to use my own things or do what I want when I want to…Oh, if only the City hadn't put such shoddy storm sewers in, we wouldn't be in this position." Her voice trailed off, and I put my arms around her, not knowing what else to do.

My parents, Paul & Katherine, newly engaged.

*First home in
Sioux City.*

Ready to dance.

*Juliana & "Sonny"
ready to play.*

Grandmother Nell Sturges.

Juliana at eleven.

TEEN YEARS
DENISON

DENISON

Our move to Grandma's house and to her ways of doing things was not difficult, at least to my eleven-year-old perceptions. The town itself was charming in a typical Midwestern way with spacious green lawns, tree-lined streets and lots of two-story houses. Most of the houses had porches where neighbors sat to capture a cool breeze on a hot summer night.

Denison was a county seat, which meant the Courthouse was located there in a park-like setting of neatly mowed grass and tall elm trees. The population in 1932 was around four thousand people. Main Street, where most of the town's retail businesses were located, led in an unbroken line from the courthouse. There was a two-story department store, Brodersons, where the money for purchases—men's shirts and suits, underwear, ladies' ready to wear—was tucked neatly into oblong metal containers and whizzed on metal wires to an upstairs office. I loved to watch those cylinders whisking back and forth, conveying money to its rightful destination.

There was a *KANDY KITCHEN*, where ice cream and candies were sold, a handy location because the movie theater was next door. I remember a photographer's studio, a hotel, a shoe store, a grocery that delivered food as well as selling it over the counter; a separate butcher shop where I sometimes went with Dad when he did the weekend shopping for Mother. It was at the shoe store where I first had my intuitive warning of sexual danger. Maybe I had sent out some encouraging signals to the young salesman who held my foot in his warm hands as I tried on a new pair of school shoes when I was in ninth grade. When he invited me to go back into the storage area so he could "look more fully" at his stock, and hoisted me up on the counter, trickles of alarm ran down my spine. I slid off the counter and ran home. After that, I always took someone with me when I went to try on shoes.

Mother felt the changes caused by the move more than anyone (beside Grandma, I now think). Mother's relationship with her mother had always had a teeter-totter quality: fear of Grandma's temper and displeasure on one end balanced by love and admiration on the other. After all, we were the "poor relations" who, while ostensibly doing grandma a favor by living with her after Grandpa died, were really by circumstances forced to move in with her. It was a downward step for Mother, and though she had many friends in the area who greeted her enthusiastically, she felt the lowering of her position.

Mother was the buffer, always cautioning us children to "behave" so as to not offend Grandma. Sonny was not to yell too loudly in the house and always remember to bring wood for the cast iron range in the kitchen. I must keep my room neat and my bed made and never forget the proper way to set the table in the dining room where all our evening meals were eaten. My special summer chores were to clean the birdbath at least once a week, and weed the Lilly of the Valley bed or whatever grew in that spot as the hot days progressed. Both chores I hated: the birdbath was slimy to scour, the flowerbed dirty and disheveled. I'm afraid I was sometimes rather sullen about those duties, and in retrospect I can see that really not much was asked of me.

I didn't mind setting the table, spreading out the tablecloth and placing the linen napkins (changed weekly on Sundays) in their initialed silver napkin rings—maybe putting a fresh bouquet of flowers in the center. After dinner Mother and I did the dishes: Mother washed, and I dried with absorbent cream-colored flour sack dishtowels. That was a time for gossip and information exchange: what Helen Ann had said when she saw her boyfriend with another girl, what to wear to school tomorrow, and the Latin homework I must do later.

Breakfast and lunch were eaten in the kitchen, except on the Friday mornings when Mrs. Brasky, the cleaning lady, came. Then it was the dining room for breakfast. It would never do for Mrs. Brasky, a tall husky woman clad in a black dress and colored apron, to find us eating in the kitchen!

Winters were a different story. Grandma made a practice of visiting her son, Jim, and his family during the winter months of the year to escape the Iowa cold. Uncle Jim, Aunt Jeanne and cousin Betty Jane, lived in a large two-story house in Houston, Texas, which had a much milder winter climate. Aunt Jeanne doted on Grandma who basked in the attention bestowed on her. I was often treated to accounts of my cousin's superior qualities—her fine grades, her thoughtfulness, her virtuosity on the piano. Mostly, I could shrug off the comparisons for I had just started piano lessons; my grades were good and besides she was a year older than I! I liked Betty Jane, and looked forward to the boxes of hand-down clothes my cousin had outgrown sent to me occasionally by Aunt Jeanne.

Because of these excursions of Grandma's, our family life took on a much more relaxed tone when she was away. We never ate in the dining room, for instance, preferring instead the cozy warmth of the kitchen where the black cast iron range gave off pleasant warmth while my brothers and I teased and joked with one another, laughing as much as we wanted to at mealtime. On the weekend, when Dad was home we often lingered at the table while Dad told us of his travels during the week.

I liked the North Brick School, the first one I attended in Denison, which was two blocks from our house, and the friends I found there. I sat in the front row of desks in the classroom, quick to raise my hand in response to questions. I remember one boy, DeVere Carey, who sat behind me and liked to surreptitiously pull at my red-brown shoulder length hair when the teacher wasn't looking. I never thought of that as a sign of boyish affection, but perhaps it was. Boys did not interest me particularly in sixth grade. When I was new in the class, two of my friends had told me of a couple in the same grade "doing it", but I couldn't imagine such a thing and refused to think about it. My only response had been a heart-felt "Ugh!"

Most of that sixth grade school year was uneventful, but a couple of things made an impression on me that still affect some of my attitudes. The first was the weekly weighing-in, heralded by the school nurse wheeling a large balance scale into the room on Friday mornings. Each student had to stand on it to be measured and weighed. The nurse called out the pounds in what seemed to me unnaturally loud tones, while the teacher kept track in a notebook. I had grown rapidly that year; had begun menstruating during the summer and had reached almost my adult height of 5'4" but had not yet shed my prepubescent fat. I weighed in at 104 pounds; more than any one else in the class except for Charles Shives, a fourteen-year-old who had endured sixth grade a number of times. It was a humiliating experience for me, and the first time I had ever thought of myself as too heavy. I recall sitting on the steel merry-go-round in the playground feeling alone and different from my friends, the cold metal chilling my bare legs in the March wind. For the rest of the school year, I felt big and clumsy, but by the time I entered seventh grade the following fall, I had lost weight in the summer due to a weeklong siege of Trench mouth accompanied by fever. Suddenly many of my friends had caught up with me and extra pounds were no longer an issue.

Trying out for glee club was traumatic too. I remember attempting mightily and self-consciously to sing the do-re-me of the scale, and failing miserably, always a little flat. I was never to attain the status of glee club member, though I was in the Presbyterian Church's Youth Choir. Churches were more forgiving of off-key singers than public schools.

By the end of the school year, life had settled into the pattern it would assume for the next nine years; years in which our country and family weathered the Great Depression in the best way we could.

DÉJÀ VU

I've only recently begun to think what it must have been like for Grandma Sims when our whole family moved into her house. Certainly she must have welcomed the thought of family life surrounding her again after the silence of widowhood. But certainly too the adjustment to the noise of children running up the stairs, or the shouts of my brothers and me in the excitement of a game, may have made her long for her former peace and quiet. In any event, here we were and we all made the best of it.

I remember my delight in having a room of my own for the first time. I could close the door on curious and teasing brothers and sit at the triple-mirrored dressing table to brush my bobbed auburn hair or, unobserved, apply bleaching lemon juice to the freckles on my nose. There was a matching ivory painted chest of drawers on which I carefully centered an embroidered doily. A special bottle of perfume seeped lavender scent into the air when I dabbed it behind my ears. A small bookcase against the wall contained a complete set of Dickens, and a tiny closet had been built out from the wall, like a shoebox on end, where I could hang my clothes. The closet was clearly an

---

afterthought, for there was no door. A limp curtain hung from wooden rings to protect its contents. The bed, with its hollowed-out center from years of use, dumped me squarely in the middle where I slept the rocklike sleep of adolescence. In summer the low windows looked out on the upper branches of the pie cherry tree; in winter the warped frames often admitted a sifting of snow into the room.

I had always loved Grandma Sims. When she visited us in Sioux City, I never failed to curl into bed with her in the mornings where she told me wonderful stories of her girlhood in Illinois. The anticipation of those visits and the golden moments of the stories are with me still. I could picture Grandma ice-skating on the Rock River in Rockford, Illinois with her brothers, red-cloaked and white-muffed; could imagine her flashing blue eyes when occasion arose for her as a young teacher to discipline one of the big farm boys in her one room school.

"I just stared at them," she would say, straightening her five-foot frame as ramrod erect in her seventies as it had been at eighteen. "They didn't dare disobey me!" I never doubted her for a second.

During the summer, while our family made plans for the move, Mother had tried to prepare me for life in Denison.

"You'll like having your own room, Dedie. You're too old now to share with the boys. You'll make new friends and you can take piano lessons. I know Sioux City is larger, but life in a small town can be lots of fun. Remember, I lived there when I was your age—I know what it's like. But people can be mean too, and they gossip a lot. Everybody

knows everyone else's business—I always hated that!"
I didn't know what she meant—what would I do that it
wouldn't be all right for others to know about?

Sometimes Mother cried that summer, making me feel
uneasy; wanting to comfort her and not knowing how.

"Why are you sad?" I asked.

"It's just that I hate to leave my own home. I never
thought I'd have to go back and live with Grandma. She
can be so cross! You don't know. You children are going
to have to be very careful to do everything she wants—
everything! It's not going to be our house you know. It's
Grandma's."

Things were different after the move, but not too much
so for us children. We never ate dinner in the kitchen any
more, as we had in Sioux City, Mother stepping easily from
stove to table to serve meals; the peony bush blooming
pinkly out the window in the summer. Now we had our
dinners in the dining room, where I set the table each night.
Grandma sat upright at the head of the oval table, Mother
opposite her except for weekends when Daddy assumed
that position. We children flanked either side. That wasn't
bad. We held our knives and forks just so to cut meat—only
one way was acceptable—the same as Mother had taught
us. One of my earliest memories is of a book cartooning
the unfortunate effects of bad manners: cocoa spilling all
over a white tablecloth because the spoon had been left in
the cup was the most graphic. The ultimate disgrace, that
seemed to me. We knew about manners, and correct grammar. Mother had learned well from her mother.

What was hard were the rules that we not giggle at
the table and that we must be excused by Grandma before

we could rise from our chairs to go out to play. Grownups took so long to eat! They chewed deliberately and talked a lot while slowly spooning their dessert of custard or pie. That was when the giggles set in. Bob, aged five, had mastered the art of flaring his nostrils and looking cross-eyed simultaneously, while carefully shading the visible side of his face with his hand. Sonny could mutter *sotto voce* a funny line well outside Grandma's limited hearing range. I struggled with paroxysms of suppressed laughter rising like an erupting Vesuvius within me, often leaving the table with new-moon welts in my palms from fingernails dug into them in an effort to maintain control. Each night was the same. I longed for escape, for the unparalleled relief of exploding with pent-up emotion.

Of all the years we spent at Grandma's, that is what I remember most about those interminable meals. That, and the time Dad got up tight-lipped from the table and stalked into the kitchen. Grandma sat quiet and stone faced while Mother pushed food around her plate with her fork. I stared at my carrots and the smell of the brown gravy on the mashed potatoes made me turn my head away. I didn't know what to do about Dad's anger. I'd never seen his temper before. It made me uncomfortable and a little frightened. Mother said later it was because Grandma made a remark about his being "only a salesman."

Now I think how difficult it must have been for all the adults. Dad, frustrated because he could not provide a large enough home for his family; Mother feeling keenly her "poor relation" status along with her loss of power. Grandma—what did she feel? Did she miss the quiet and order of her home after so many years of rearing a family of her own? Surely her strength and patience had reached its zenith years before. She bore her own recent widowhood stoically. I never thought of it. After all, Grandpa had been eighty when he died; that was old. Once I heard Grandma say to Mother,

"How Papa would have loved..." and stopped. Both she and Mother had tears in their eyes and I looked away.

After we moved into the Denison house, a subtle change took place between Grandma and me. Maybe I was too big to crawl into bed with her anymore—perhaps the novelty wore off, or I shrugged my shoulders impatiently at an embrace. In any case, Grandma took on a more supervisory role.

"Have you practiced the piano today, Juliana? Cousin Betty Jane practices an hour every day. She plays very well."

Betty Jane, who was an only child, did everything perfectly. I consoled myself with the thought that she was, after all, a year older and had an edge on me.

Also, there were the chores that Grandma imposed, not Mother. The house rules about rising and sleeping times. I didn't feel special to Grandma any more.

Last night I watched two of my grandchildren at the dinner table. They wolfed down their food in order to eat the candy Easter eggs I brought them. I wanted to plunk David in his chair, force him to use his silverware instead of stuffing food in his mouth with his fingers. I yearned to tell Emily that sitting at the table with her knees under her chin while she ate was far from the correct posture for a young lady. I wanted them both to sit quietly, eat properly, get nourishment from their food instead of jumping up and down, running from the table at will, burning up the calories as soon as they were taken into their thin little bodies. I wanted them to stop talking, demanding their mother's attention constantly; quiet their shrill giggling. I told David to stop twirling about as he ate his candy; held my tongue as he continued gyrating about the room

There was nothing I could say.

Suddenly, I wished I could talk with Grandma Sims.

First Love

In the spring of seventh grade I fell madly in love. This was different than the giggling I'd been doing over one of the boys in eighth grade who was sweet on my cousin, writing him notes and then tearing them into tiny pieces to scatter in the wind, but that was a fantasy kind of thing. The idea of actually talking to a boy other than my brothers or Earl Lee who lived down the street and just hung around, was as scary to me as the creaking gate on *Inner Sanctum* on the radio Thursday nights.

Falling in love happens suddenly, without warning, and that's the way it was with me on that warm May afternoon in Denison, Iowa on my way home from school. Walking along the cracked sidewalk on a street where the homes were modest single story clapboard structures, not like the two story houses on the street where my family lived with Grandma in this year of 1934, I saw a *PUPPIES FOR SALE* sign nailed to a tree, crudely lettered in crayon on a piece of brown cardboard. An arrow pointed to the back of the house and I walked the grassy driveway as though pulled by a magnet.

"Come to see the puppies?" the woman who'd been

scrubbing the wooden steps of her house said, drying her hands on a corner of her apron. "Here they are. Pretty small though—won't be able to leave their mother for another few weeks."

She lifted a blanket covering half the box at her feet, to reveal a squirming bunch of puppies eagerly crowding around their mother's tits.

"They're so small," I said. "Can I hold one?"

"Not yet, come back next week. Then you can."

I stood entranced, already knowing the puppy I would choose. There were two black and white ones, an all black and a white. That was the one I wanted, that adorable white puppy, the smallest of the lot.

"What kind are they?" I asked.

"Fox terriers. Pure bred—well almost. The mother, anyway."

"How much do they cost?"

"Five dollars. A bargain for such good dogs."

She didn't have to tell me. I knew they were good. But $5.00! —that was a lot! If I saved all my allowance for the next four weeks it would only amount to $2.00. But I had a birthday coming up in June. Maybe if I could talk Mother into it—that would be the best present I could imagine.

The following week I went back, sitting on my haunches and staring wordlessly at the puppies as they rolled and squirmed, whined and yipped at their mother's side. After that it became routine for me to stop by every day on my way home from school. I was fixated on the small white dog, growing plumper each day and more fully covered with his soft white fur. When the time came, I was allowed to hold him, to stroke his back and talk softly to him.

"Your name is Snap," I said one day. "because you're always snapping at your brothers and sisters."

At home, my campaign for dog ownership was going well. Mother had bowed to the inevitable and said a dog would make a good birthday present, but I'd have to take complete responsibility: feed him, bathe him, housebreak too. I agreed to all without reservation. I would do anything for Snap!

"We're weaning the puppies now," Mrs. Slocum said one day. "You can take yours home next week."

The following Friday, I pressed five one-dollar bills, sticky with perspiration, into Mrs. Slocum's hand, and held the squirming puppy against my chest. "Come on Snap, it's time to go home. I've got a nice box all ready for you, and some good food too."

For the next three weeks, Snap and I were inseparable. He was pulled in the wagon, watched over with tender concern as he gobbled the special meals I prepared for him: leftover oatmeal from breakfast, some stew from last night's dinner. I even got the butcher to give me some bones." Not too big, his mouth is pretty small." I wiped up puppy puddles without complaint, placing him carefully on the newspaper I'd provided for such events. "Next time, Snappy, go here!" I said sternly, hoping I wasn't hurting his feelings. My two brothers were barely allowed to look at him, let alone touch.

"Sonny, watch out! You'll step on him!"

"Bobby, stop teasing! He's too little to play with a stick! And he is not cross-eyed!" He was, I'd discovered, but I didn't care.

I bathed my dog, toweling him dry on the sweet smelling grass of the front yard where I'd brought the washbasin of warm soapy water. I lay flat on the grass watching him sleep, or perched on one elbow while he lapped up cool water from a pristinely clean bowl. A blue ribbon adorned his white neck. Dad would bring a collar home from his next trip. Nothing was too good for my dog.

And then one morning, I fell out of love. It happened as suddenly as my former state of bliss had begun. Feeding Snap was a chore, not a benign blessing; cleaning up after him wasn't fun anymore.

"Sonny—do you want to give Snap a bath today" I'll let you this one time."

"Bobby, I guess its o.k. for you to feed the dog tonight."

After that, Snap became the family dog. Mother fed him scraps from the table: my brothers yelled 'C'mon, Boy!' as they sped to school on their bikes. I rubbed his ears and petted him, but he was no longer my exclusive property.

Snap became part of our family lore, woven into stories like the time Dad came home late on a Friday night after his week on the road. Mother thought he was arriving on Saturday so she locked the house and went to bed and Dad was forced to climb in through a basement window. Snap didn't even growl at him.

"Some watchdog," Dad said.

The funny part of it was that I didn't really learn how easy it was to fall in and out of love. That was a lesson I had to repeat many times.

CHRISTMAS SWEETS

In Denison, in the 1930's Mother started making candy for the Christmas boxes early in December. It was a project she loved and to which she gave all her energy for the next two weeks. Her specialty was fondant, sweet and creamy, colored and variously flavored. Her preliminary efforts lay in getting the toppings for the candy prepared: blanched almonds; perfect walnut halves, small squares of citron and some candied cherries. Bob, Sonny and I watched her slipping the skins from blanched almonds and knew what lay ahead.

"Mom, will you wait till after supper to cook the fondant?" we'd ask, knowing the drama of the process and not wanting to miss it while we were in school.

"Well, maybe I can put it off till then," she'd say, a calculating look in her eyes. "You know we have to let it ripen for a week. I'll have to figure out my time schedule."

She always let us watch. Part of the fun when the sugar and water mixture came to a boil in the big kettle was seeing the carefully measured cream of tartar gently tapped into the mixture with the resultant foaming up of the pan's contents, almost to the top, then back again. Then, the patient waiting and watching as the mix boiled and Mother poured small drops into a cup of cold water, gently stirring with her finger to see if the drops formed a soft ball. "A little longer," she'd say, and finally, "I think its just right!"

We'd stand a little aside, as she lifted the kettle and gently poured the hot liquid onto a marble slab, where it was allowed to cool. Then with a flat-sided wooden spoon, she would begin working the mass, turning it into itself over and over like kneading bread dough, until it became opaque and creamy and she was satisfied with its texture.

"All right. Now I'll put it away until we're ready to color and shape it", she'd say as she dumped the fondant into a large bowl and covered it with a plate. I knew the timing for the next step would coincide with Dad's arrival home on the weekend. In the meantime, Mother had put all the carefully prepared toppings into their separate containers and gotten out the supply of boxes in which we would carefully place the candies so they could be wrapped and shipped to far away members of the family in time for Christmas.

By Saturday evening, each of us, Dad included, sat at the kitchen table with a different colored and flavored— pink for peppermint, green for pistachio and so on—wax paper covered roll of fondant on a plate in front of him. We each cut off small sections of the candy, rolled it between our palms and put the balls on a sheet of wax paper near each place. Then came the fun of selecting a proper topping to squish down atop the center of each ball of candy to flatten and decorate it. Here were all of Mother's carefully prepared garnishes, the nuts, candied fruit, and pieces of citron. Our motions became automatic, with an occasional comment as to technique.

"Sonny, you're putting the almonds on *crooked.* They're supposed to be in the middle! Bobby, stop licking your fingers—it's not sanitary!" I was, after all, the elder sister who had to keep track of proper procedure and not loath to correct my brothers.

Dad would clear his throat and begin reminiscences about his week away from home calling on customers. He'd tell us about the heavy snowfall in Nebraska or a joke someone told him. Or maybe he'd start a long story about his Uncle Bill in Winner, South Dakota. Uncle Bill, a widower, was raising four boys and a daughter and they managed to get into more scrapes than any family I'd ever heard of. Years later, Dad was to gather all those stories into a biography of Uncle Bill and sell it to the *American Magazine.* Uncle Bill himself would be interviewed on a popular radio show called *We the People.* The story ended up in a high school literature textbook as an example of well-written biography. But all that was in the future, about which we knew nothing. Mother had heard many of the tales before but she always laughed as though it were the first time.

On those cold, snowy December nights we sat cozily in the kitchen, warmed by the wood range, and assembled hundreds of fondant candies, packing them carefully in layers in the cardboard boxes saved throughout the year. The boxes, wrapped in red or green tissue paper, then in sturdy brown paper, were sent off to our relatives. Sometimes Mother made Divinity candy too, or a batch of fudge to fill out the boxes. One year she experimented with dipping the fondant in chocolate. My favorite combination was the sticky Medjool dates from California stuffed with pistachio flavored fondant

Making that candy was a hedge against the Depression, which threatened dad's income constantly. Sending gifts of candy to relatives was an inexpensive way to remember them.

There were other economies: We children were used to saving on the electric bill by sitting in the dark while listening to the radio. Our meals often consisted of creamed codfish or chipped beef on toast, which we ate voraciously with no thought of deprivation. New clothes were a rarity. We didn't consider ourselves deprived, though I sometimes envied my more affluent girlfriends whose wardrobes were more extensive than mine.

Other holiday treats were dark fruitcakes filled with candied cherries, nuts, citron and candied pineapple; plum puddings made with suet, citron and dark raisins, steamed in a greased coffee can and served with vanilla flavored hard sauce for Christmas dinner. Mincemeat too was a favorite and not the store bought variety of today, but the real thing made with chopped cooked meat and all the other flavorful and cholesterol-filled ingredients handed down from our English forebears. I don't make any of these things today, in our health conscious world, but I did when my children were small and burning up every calorie I put into them.

The food preparation that my own children loved to take part in usually centered around harvest fruits. Canning apricots and garlic dill pickles were two favorites. I remembered the careful placing of apricots in jars when I worked in the Del Monte cannery in the summer of 1942, and quickly realized the value of small fingers and hands for this task. Jimmy, Cathy and Joan took great pleasure in competing for the best layering of the golden halves, while Judy and I cut the ripe fruit from a neighbor's tree into halves, working fast so as to keep up with their nimble fingers.

The children loved making dill pickles too and there was a lot of noisy competition to see who could do the most jars. We'd set up an assembly line at the kitchen table, with glass Mason jars in a row, sliced cucumbers in a big bowl and stalks of fresh dill leaning against the wall or on the table. There were garlic cloves too, and bay leaves. One year we put up twenty-five quarts of dill pickles, and managed to eat them all before the next year's cucumbers were ripe for pickling. My version became so popular that I unashamedly named them for myself, and will close this chapter with the recipe.

JULIANA'S GARLIC DILLS

Four pounds pickling cucumbers, 4-5 inches long.
Six tablespoons salt
1 1/2 tablespoons mustard seed
3 cups white vinegar
3 cups water
Garlic cloves, peeled
Packaged Dill seed, if fresh dill not available.
6 bay leaves

Wash cucumbers. Combine salt, mustard seed, vinegar and water. Heat to boiling. Pack cucumbers into sterilized jars (Not necessary if using hot water bath method). Add a clove of garlic to each jar and if using fresh dill, stuff as much of it as possible into jar. Fill with boiling vinegar solution. Add 2 T. dill seed and one bay leaf to each jar. Seal jars and process in hot water bath for ten minutes. Makes six pints (or maybe quarts—I don't remember).

The Yellow Bathing Suit

A nn Mary was doing it again. I watched under my half closed eyelids as she squealed,

"Help me, please!" holding up her arms in a helpless gesture from the warm water of the swimming pool in Denison. "I can't get out by myself."

Three boys came running and grasped her outstretched hands to pull my cousin from the pool. I could see the water ballooning from the cups of her yellow rubber bathing suit, almost revealing the nipples of her ample breasts. Could see, too, the boys' eager expressions, their sideways glances at her bosom.

It wasn't fair! Why should Ann Mary get to have the only real rubber bathing suit in Denison? What was so great about a rubber suit anyway? It just looked like her bathing cap of the same latex material, embossed with the diamond and flower pattern. I knew it was because she got to live in Chicago and could shop there where they had exotic things. Why should she get such a nice tan, while I only burned and peeled and got freckles? Why should the boys pay so much attention to her and none to me?

It was the summer of our fourteenth year, and Ann

Mary and her brother Jack were staying for two months at Grandma's house. Just because they didn't have a mother since Aunt Patty died, didn't seem an adequate reason to me to have to watch Ann Mary and the boys who clustered around her for two whole months! She looked so silly, glancing at them sideways from under her lowered eyelashes, or pouting a little with her full red lips. Where had she learned to act like that? Did living in Chicago make you grow up sooner? Last summer, when we were thirteen, had been different. She'd been more like me then, wanting to be with my girlfriends, or go to the movies and the library. But this year was different. There were all these boys, and that darned bathing suit!

Though I didn't realize it at the time, I was embarking on a learning experience very different from my studies in school. It began last summer, but I hardly noticed, this feeling that someone else had something I didn't. For the first time in my life I had to share the attention that heretofore had been mine alone as the only girl in our family. I had to watch my brothers tease Ann Mary as well as me, see Grandma giving her special little pats on the shoulder and watch Mother beam as Ann Mary and Jack devoured her wonderful lemon meringue pies. Didn't Mother know we loved those pies as much as they did, even if we didn't talk about them so often?

I had to admit it was fun to have Ann Mary to walk downtown with, hastily and daringly applying lipstick when we'd reached the corner and were out of sight of the house. Grandma wouldn't like us to use lipstick, even if it was only Tangee and just made our own lip color seem brighter. And it was fun to giggle over Bud Pautch and the way he came over faithfully every night just to talk to my cousin as she sat in the wooden slat swing on the screened in front porch. He hung around looking at her from outside, rubbing his forefinger on the screened door and talking in a low voice.

"He says he's going to write me every day next year! I'll bet he won't—I'm not going to answer every letter!"

The next summer, when we were fifteen, was different. Ann Mary was sickly that year, with boils on her legs that had to be bandaged all the time and made it hard for her to walk, she said. The community swimming pool was off limits until she was healed. During the beastly heat of July and August, while she read her book in the shade of the big elm tree, I spent my time fetching a stool and pillow so she could rest her leg, running for glasses of lemonade and steadying her on my arm while she hopped to the bathroom.

"It's so nice out here, and I can talk to people when they walk by," she said. "Why don't you bring your book out too?"

"When I get my chores done, I will. I have to clean the birdbath and make our bed first." It was hard, being the healthy one, not glamorous at all. I wished I could have a little of my cousin's pallor, much more interesting than her tan of last year. My own cheeks, I thought, were too pink to be interesting.

But it was fun when the two of us played double solitaire in the afternoons when we were having our "rest" time. Mother had introduced us to the game, setting up a card table in her bedroom upstairs, and laughing with us as we struggled to win. Mother liked Ann Mary, especially when she raved about her pies and biscuits and I guessed that was all right with me since my cousins probably didn't get very good food at home with no mother to cook for them. And I really was glad that the infected leg was almost healed by the end of August when it was time for my cousins to go back to Chicago, and spend the school year with Uncle Alan, my favorite uncle.

As the summer of my sixteenth year approached, I began to worry. The refrain "sweet sixteen and never been kissed" ran through my head all spring, and I dreaded Ann Mary's visit which I knew would be replete with her tales of "necking" with Johnny, her Chicago boyfriend. I would have no answering stories of my own to report: I'd still be just plain, unsophisticated, unkissed, "Dedie" for another summer.

I needn't have worried, though, for the tide was about to turn. Instead of my cousins' annual visit in Denison, I was invited to be a guest in Uncle Alan's new home in Oak Park, a suburb on the north side of Chicago. I would travel by myself on the train, get to plan the right clothes for a two-week visit, have an adventure!

Tides had turned for Uncle Alan that year as well. In March he'd married again, a woman named Esther. Aunt Esther was a short, plump woman with dark hair and brown eyes and an enchanting way of laughing with her tongue peeking through the small gap between her front teeth. I loved the way she listened to us with intent brown eyes or sat giggling softly at our girlish stories after a shopping spree in Chicago's "loop" where we'd wandered through *Marshall Fields* and *Carson, Pirie, Scott* sampling perfumes and lipsticks at the cosmetic counters, trying on hats in the millinery department. She laughed at my amazement at the speed of the "El" that whisked us downtown before I had time to peer curiously into the windows of the tenements we passed on the journey.

"Those apartment buildings looked so tall, and so dirty! I didn't know people lived like that!" I said soberly.

Best of all during that two-week visit, though, were the boys! Suddenly there were automobile horns honking outside the house on the warm summer evenings, boys at the wheel that my cousin knew.

"Go for a ride?" they'd yell and with permission from Uncle Alan, we were allowed to go joyriding for a couple of hours, circling the streets slowly while the boys nonchalantly pointed out landmarks to me, the visitor. The boys seemed to think I was special—I was "the new girl in town" this summer.

My springtime worry of reaching this momentous age labeled "sweet sixteen and never been kissed" vanished in the backseat of a convertible with a boy named Johnny Metz, whose dark hair and eyes and wide smile captured my all-too-willing heart. We kissed exuberantly and I found I needed little practice in this new art.

"Hasta la vista," he would say each evening as he left me at the door. "I'll see you soon." And on the last night, "I'll write you if you'll answer my letters."

Oh, that was a glorious vacation! I had caught up with Ann Mary at last!

Dancing Daughter

My love for dancing certainly did not begin with my first lessons in the art. Those first instructions took place in a summer school class in tap dancing when I was just out of fifth grade. My feet seemed independent of the signals my brain tried to send them and flopped awkwardly at the ends of my legs like puppets out of control. No matter how I tried to tap as the instructor told us, I was off beat and the butt of sniggering from my classmates. At the end of the six-week session, the only thing I had to show for the experience was a pair of used tap shoes Mother had managed to purchase from someone. I was glad to forget about anything rhythmic involving my body for the next several years.

But time and life in the thirties had a way of involving young people in the art of dancing—ballroom dancing, that is. The movies were full of it from the *Ziegfield Follies* to the famous Rogers and Astaire team. We knew and sang all the popular songs, such as *"Blue Moon"* and *"Wrap Your Troubles in Dreams"*.

My first real introduction to dancing, other than mother giving me a few rudiments of the steps, came about because

I joined Rainbow Girls. This was a somewhat exclusive organization of young ladies of Protestant background. I forget what the significance of the term "Rainbow Girls" was, but I do remember we had to memorize extensive parts of secret ritual. There was a definite hierarchy of status, the top of which was the chief Rainbow Girl. Needless to say, I started out in the lowest position, that of guardian of the outer doors.

We all wore white dresses. Mine was white dotted Swiss, with a sash and a long skirt. I loved getting dressed up in it, perhaps because of my early conditioning by Mother when she told me I would wear such garments when I grew up. In any event, I guarded the door until I was finally promoted to a still lowly, but inside station in the inner sanctum. It was there I discovered my true nature, or at least an aspect of it, when I found I could not recite the solemn three sentence part I had to say, without bursting into uncontrollable mirth. Nor did my irreverence stop at my own doorstep: I couldn't understand how the older girls could recite such serious declarations and vows with a straight face. I dreaded the meetings, but already knew there was a bonus at the end of the evening so I controlled my feelings as best I could.

The bonus was the DeMolay boys, who belonged to a similar organization, which met on the same night. After their respective meetings, the Rainbow Girls and the DeMolay boys gathered in the downstairs social hall of the building, where we had refreshments and danced. It must have been pretty clumsy dancing, for none of us had had the benefit of any formal training. Probably most had been briefed by their mothers, as I had. But we'd all seen Ginger Rogers and Fred Astaire in their wonderful dancing movies, and we knew how we were supposed to look. We knew the proper position, girl's left hand on boy's right shoulder, right and left hands respectively clasped, sometimes damp with nervous perspiration. Our mothers had taught us the waltz steps:*one* two, three, *one*, two, three —and the foxtrot—*feet make a box to the count of four.* The record player scratched out *The Blue Danube, Tea for Two,* and we proceeded around the floor in pairs. I began to get the hang of moving to the music; my feet obeyed better than they had with tap shoes on them. Over several months of practice, we all began to feel more at ease and to experiment with a few new steps.

In ninth grade my first High School dance —the Freshman Fall Fling—took place. It was a big event. I went with several of my girlfriends, Dad depositing the carload of giggling girls outside the gymnasium, with the promise that he'd return in a couple of hours.

Inside, sitting on the wooden bleachers, I waited nervously with my friends for a partner to appear, while across the room the boys clumped awkwardly in their Sunday shoes, casting sideways glances at us. Finally one of the boys, like an errant cell breaking away from a cluster, crossed the floor to find a partner. Others followed and soon I was partnered with a boy a head taller than myself. I tried to make conversation as he frowned in concentration, counting lightly under his breath. During one of the steps I inadvertently trod on my own foot, thereby untying a shoelace and in an agony of embarrassment tried for the rest of the number to avoid tripping on it. I prayed fervently that my partner would not notice its trailing presence, or trip on it himself. I thought the music would never end.

However, more practice and my own enthusiasm helped my confidence. Mother suggested I give a boy-girl party in the spring of that freshman year, and I did inviting a dozen or so friends. We pulled back the rugs, put on some music and danced, with Mother giving instructions to some of the less initiated. One of the girls she helped was Donnabelle Mullenger, the prettiest girl in school and a neighborhood friend. Donnabelle stayed with her grandmother, a few doors from us, during the school year because her family lived on a too-distant farm outside of town. She was to be May Queen that spring, and was also starring in the annual school play.

"She's a bit heavy on her feet, ", Mother said, and I took comfort from that assessment, for it was difficult not to be a little jealous of someone as pretty and smart and nice as Donnabelle. Little did any of us dream that my friend would go on to become the famous movie star, Donna Reed. To me she was always Donnabelle.*

As in many Iowa towns, there was a large dancehall on its outskirts. Denison's was called *The Uwana*, and during the summer months different bands played each week. Occasionally Lawrence Welk, a South Dakotan, brought his Rippling Rhythm to the floor and once Tommy Dorsey came, along with Betty Hutton who belted out her signature song *A Tisket, A Tasket* in her inimitable frenetic style.

At the end of my sophomore year, I begged to be allowed to go to the *Uwana* on summer evenings. Mother and Dad, dubious as they must have been, decided to take a friend and me one evening to check it out. Apparently the dance hall met their approval because from then on I was allowed to go with friends to dance a couple of nights a week. I was easily the most enthusiastic of any of my cohorts, who may have been better on the basketball court or the track team, but couldn't keep up with me on the dance floor. I thrived on dancing with different partners, learning to follow their steps and trying out new ones like the *Shag, Lindy Hop,* and *Jitterbug.*

Little did I suspect then that the ability to follow a partner's steps without thought would often stand me in good stead in my life. Or finally force me to take the lead on my own.

*Donna Reed did become a very big Hollywood star, acting in many movies and winning an Academy Award for her portrayal of Lorene, a "lady of the evening" in the movie *From Here to Eternity.*

Denison, Iowa, is very proud of its Hollywood star and has festivals every year in her memory.

GUILT

I am good at guilt. Even though I wasn't raised Catholic, the religion that is said to major in that subject, my Protestant upbringing gave me enough do's and don'ts for leading a sinless life to qualify me as an expert.

The first instance I can recall is one that taught me how guilt can gnaw at the innards, spoiling all it comes into contact with. It went like this:

Occasionally Mother would ask me to stop at the Piggly Wiggly store on my way home from school to purchase something she needed for our supper, such as a loaf of bread or a stalk of celery. One day, giving me a dime to put in my pocket she said,

"Dedie, I need a head of cabbage for our dinner tonight. You can stop at the store after school and if you see any cabbage, buy it. Otherwise you can get something for yourself."

I could get something for myself! There were heart shaped pink candies at the candy counter I'd been fantasizing about for a week, imagining their smooth, cool, sweet taste yet not having the money to buy any. If only the store would be out of cabbages today I daydreamed as I practiced penmanship that afternoon. But they would probably have it, I thought. Chances of the Piggly Wiggly being out of cabbages were slim, and I resigned myself to carrying home a round head of the vegetable in a paper sack after school.

But wait—Mother had said if I *saw* any cabbage I was to buy it. What if I didn't see that particular item? Would I be cheating to buy candy instead?

The idea took hold as the afternoon wore on, and by the time the school bell rang, I had decided on a course of action. I would not see any cabbage that day. Walking into the store, and keeping my gaze sternly averted from the vegetable display, I marched directly to the candy counter.

"I'll take five of those, and five of the chocolate ones," I said to the clerk, pointing out my choices. My heart raced with excitement, and I ran nearly all the way home, clutching the bag of candy in my sweaty palm.

"I didn't see any cabbages at the store today," I sang out to Mother as I came in the house, and went directly to my bedroom where I emptied out the contents of the bag on the bedspread. There they were, all ten pieces of candy, mine! I popped one in my mouth. It was disappointedly bland in flavor. Somehow, I'd lost my appetite for confectionaries that day.

The yearning didn't come back, either. As the days went on, just the thought of that illicitly gained treasure began to nauseate me. How could I have fibbed so to Mother? Was it so bad, what I'd done? After all, I hadn't *seen* any cabbage that day! But I knew the truth, and I knew what would ease my conscience.

"Mommy, I have something to tell you," I confessed

one day when the dark cloud of guilt threatened to engulf me, and I told her the story.

"That was pretty foolish of you, wasn't it?" Mother said as she wiped away my tears. "It wasn't really worth it all, was it?"

Of course it wasn't and the discomfort of keeping a guilty secret did not leave me for many years. It was just easier to tell the truth.

Of course, as I got into my teens, sometimes omission of facts was easier to deal with than the unvarnished truth, though I didn't think of that as actually lying. Most of my sins of omission concerned Grandma Sims, whose standards were strict and I thought out of date. She didn't need to know I'd gone to a movie on a Sunday afternoon instead of visiting a girlfriend as I'd let her assume, or the reason I had peppermint on my breath was because I'd had a cigarette after school at *Louie's* where my friends and I met every day.

It wasn't until I met Bill Kness that I began lying to Mother. Not at first of course, because then I could tell her how exciting and good looking he was. She could see that for herself when he came to visit, and took me on dates in his father's big black Oldsmobile. She could see the flush in my cheeks, the lightness in my step that last year of high school when Bill and I were inseparable as much of the time as possible, seeing that he lived in another town and had to drive twenty miles to visit me.

What she didn't know, I thought, was that I was beginning to lie to her. I didn't tell the truth about the lateness of the hour I came home some evenings; I didn't tell her how Bill was beginning to press me to "show how much I loved him" and that I, fearful of losing him, had yielded, timidly at first but with increasing enthusiasm. Didn't tell her about the tacit approval I'd gotten from God after the first time when I asked Him to give me a sign if what I was doing was wrong, and had not received one. Was I the same girl who didn't *see* the cabbage? I think so.

And then, after high school graduation and the beginning of summer and bouts with nausea and other signs, and more lies, I had to face the truth. I had to tell my parents that I was pregnant; that Bill would marry me and that is what we'd do.

The worst part of it all was the guilt I felt at betraying the trust my parents had placed in me. The best part, in the end, was the darling baby daughter I had the following March, whom we named Judith Ann Kness. I hadn't known how wonderful and all-consuming my love for a child would be, how her presence in my life was a never-ending joy.

But my guilt was not erased with Judy's birth. Even though my parents never said a word of reproach, that guilt and of course shame, hung over me for years. I couldn't forgive myself; even though I could accept that God had long ago done so. For twenty years, not a day passed that I didn't remember how my father's voice had thickened with emotion when he learned I was pregnant. I was responsible for that quick sadness in him, which went away as suddenly, and the remembrance skewered me each time I thought of it.

In those days, it was always the girl's responsibility to keep her reputation unsullied; to remain virginal until she was married and if that was not the case, to keep from becoming pregnant. When the unthinkable happened, it was she about whom it was said, with an ill concealed superiority, "she's made her bed; now she's got to lie in It". It was the woman whose reputation was forever sullied by her mistake. Memories in small towns are very long.

And so I lied. I was not brave enough, as I would be today, to state my predicament boldly. I told my friends Bill and I had been secretly married in the summertime, not in December with just both sets of parents present, which was actually the case. As time went on, and Bill and I divorced, our family moved away from Denison to settle in California, where the necessity for lies became less and less, but always I carried that deep burden of shame and guilt within me. I grew adept at assuming the mantle of a carefree college student, and was always proud to talk about Judy and her adorable ways to anyone I thought interested. But deep in my heart I felt I didn't quite measure up to the picture I presented to the world.

It all seems rather silly now, in light of today's mores: the lack of judgment by society on such an occurrence, the commonality of pregnant brides walking confidently down the aisle to take wedding vows.

I look back today on the young girl I was and try to understand how she could have been so foolish. And then I think about the times we were in, the hopelessness the Depression had engendered in me, the tight finances of our family. Mother talked about my going to college, but I knew we didn't have the money. In those days, in Iowa, there were no community colleges, no student loans. One did not borrow money to finance a college education. I can almost understand a young girl's reaching out for love without much thought to the future.

Years later, I began to learn the value of reaching out, of revealing the hidden aspect of myself, and the pain subsided, along with feelings of guilt.

So why do I talk about it now? Because it is a part of who I am, the decisions I've made. The suffering and shame I experienced have made me a more understanding woman, one not so quick to judge the shortcomings of others as I might have become as I grew older. I'm a little sorry for that young girl who could not enjoy her normal sexuality without a sense of wrongdoing, but I was a product of my time as each of us is. We cannot change the influence of the peers and family values we grew up with without learning to forgive ourselves for past mistakes. For me, it has been a worthwhile effort.

WESTWARD HO

Although the months from November 1940 until spring of the next year were anxious ones for me—how could I support a baby in a town with so little prospects as Denison—things were going better for my parents. Dad had gotten a position with the largest harness and saddle manufacturing company in the country, Bona Allen of Buford, Georgia. The company made many types of leather goods, but specialized in ornate silver trimmed saddles, such as the popular film star, Leo Carrillo, rode on at the head of the Rose Parade in Pasadena each New Year's day.

Dad's territory was huge. It stretched from the Mississippi River to the Pacific Ocean. We could live anywhere he chose.

It was time to leave Denison and Grandma's house. and all the gossip a small town breeds. Grandma would be fine, she assured us, though she was nearly ninety by now. But she spent her winters in Houston with her son Jim and family, and there was plenty of help for her when she was at home.

So in June 1941, our family—Dad, Mother, Paul, Bob,

Judy and I—was on our way to California, where we would live. The prospect was exciting for all of us. Wasn't California the land of movie stars, permanent sunshine—and earthquakes? We would find a house in San Jose, he said. He'd liked that town on the two previous trips he had made there. It was just the right size and had a college Paul and I could attend.

Off we went in our new Nash four door sedan, all six of us, complete with Judy's potty-chair for sudden necessary stops along the way. It sounds impossible now, with modern rules for infant car seats and the invariable bucket seats in front. But in 1941 there were no seat belts; the front seat was ample for three people and a fifteen-month-old doesn't take much room.

We were all in good spirits. Paul, 17, and Bob, 12, were at the height of adolescent high jinks and good-natured jibes; Dad was full of funny stories. Mother and I basked in the male good humor, and we all adored and petted little Judy. I remember a stop in Yellowstone National Park where the men went fishing and caught a string of lake trout, which Mother grilled on a grate over an open fire in front of the cabin we'd rented for a night or two. No fish has ever tasted so good since!

I had never seen mountains. Both of my brothers had made trips with Dad earlier, and my parents had honeymooned at Pike's Peak. I marveled at the rushing streams, steep roads and endless vistas of forest, all different from the rolling green hills of Iowa.

There were other differences from the rolling farmlands of Iowa as well—the seemingly endless hot desert in Nevada, the Great Salt Lake in which we floated. And finally California, more mountains, Lake Tahoe, and at last San Francisco. All those houses on the sides of the hills, so clean and sparkling in the sunlight, the cable cars laboring up the hills—so many things to see!

But Dad pressed on, down El Camino Real to San Jose. "We'll find a place to stay and look around for a house to rent. We'll have time to see San Francisco later."

Dad made the decisions and we acquiesced quickly, like you do with a tour guide in a foreign city.

I still think of that first view of San Jose the next day, after a night in a motel, as we drove east on Santa Clara Street. We were headed for the Naglee Park area where there were several houses for us to look at. The eastern foothills loomed ahead; brown as they must have been in summer, but to me they were a beacon of adventure. Everything seemed beautiful and strange. I was determined to master the exotic Spanish names so foreign to my midwestern tongue.

"Not San Josay, Bob! It's San Hosay—they'll think you're a hick if you say it that way!" Bob grinned wickedly and continued to mispronounce whenever I was within earshot. *Manana—do it tomorrow*—we'd been told would be the prevailing philosophy here, and I wondered if we'd get used to that.

In San Jose we found the right house for us at the right price (about $40 a month) on South 14th St. in San Jose. It was a roomy, Craftsman style home with a full basement, three large bedrooms with walk-in closets, as well as a big living room, dining room, kitchen and service porch. In the back yard were two cherry trees, still bearing some of this year's crop, a Black Tartarian and a Royal Anne.

What bliss! We were in California at last! My brothers and I climbed a ladder to pick some cherries and Mother talked about making a pie when she got settled.

I had stumbled into adulthood with my responsibilities as a mother, but my family cushioned the shock and I was still sheltered from what could have been a very harsh reality. I probably did not fully appreciate their generosity of spirit at the time—youth has a way of accepting whatever gifts are given without a great deal of reflection.

Grandma Sims with left to right, Ann Mary and Juliana.

Juliana at seventeen.

SAN JOSE
CAMPBELL YEARS

A Bowl of Cherries

"Hey, Bob," I called to my younger brother "Pass me that basket, will you, so I can get the rest of these Royal Anne's. We've probably got enough of the Tartarians for the pie Mother's going to make."

Bob and I were standing on the roof of the house, basking in the July sunshine and picking the last ripe fruit from the two cherry trees whose branches conveniently overhung the roof. I could visualize those cream-and-pink hued Royal Annes in the blue bowl in the kitchen. These cherries were different from the ones we'd had in Denison, where they'd been small and sour. These were California cherries, plump and sweet.

I looked down into the backyard where fifteen month old Judy sat in the swing Dad had fashioned for her on the limb of one of the cherry trees. Mother was pushing her gently while Judy giggled. "Nana, more!" she commanded.

My parents were delighted with the home they found to rent on South Fourteenth Street, in the Naglee Park section of the city of San Jose. One story, flat roofed, in what seemed a typically California style, the rooms were large with built-in china cabinets in the dining room and lovely polished wood bookcases flanking the fireplace in the spacious living room. There were walk-in closets in the three bedrooms; a bathroom so large I felt you could hear an echo in it, and a full basement where Dad set up an office and put up shelves for Mother's canned goods. The service porch off the kitchen was flanked with windows on two sides and large enough to accommodate one of Mother's prized possessions, her ironing mangle. How she delighted in her neatly piled stack of still-warm sheets and pillowcases, tablecloths and napkins.

It hadn't taken long to get settled in San Jose. Mother's dining room set and her bedroom furniture had arrived soon after we moved into the house. Trips to cheap furniture stores had furnished my bedroom with a bleached oak early California style "set" and bunk beds for my brothers. I'd found a small youth bed for Judy at a thrift store. The living room was sparsely furnished in more of the California oak style so popular then. Dad's complete set of Mark Twain and John Muir books helped fill the bookcases.

We'd explored the surrounding area too. One Sunday a trip to Santa Cruz where we shivered in the ocean and cooked hamburgers on the barbeque; another weekend, a drive in the hills near Los Altos where Mother held her breath while Dad nonchalantly pointed out sights as he maneuvered the car around the steep, curvy road. Dad was apt to get carried away in the excitement of new discoveries when he drove. More than once, the car lurched erratically as he waved an arm to point out a strange bird or an unfamiliar tree.

"Oh Paul," Mother would hiss through clenched teeth.

"It's straight down the mountain on this side! Be careful!"

We'd had one trip to San Francisco. Mother and I had dressed for the city in our best dresses, hats and gloves. It had seemed to me the trip took forever as we drove up El Camino Real, slowed by the many stops along the way: Sunnyvale, Mountain View, Palo Alto, San Carlos—I couldn't remember all the names of the towns the road ran through. There was no 101 highway then skirting the shores of the Bay, no beautiful 280 winding through the foothills to make the trip shorter.

The wait had been worth it, though. I had pushed Judy in her stroller through so much of Golden Gate Park that day that my feet ached We'd gone on to Fisherman's Wharf where we ate a fish dinner and watched the gulls swoop over the water. We drove up to Coit Tower, gazing out over the city in the twilight, and finally headed for home.

"We'll ride a cable car next time," Dad promised, "and let you and Mother off at Union Square to shop."

Yes, we were getting settled in. My brother Paul and I would enroll at San Jose State in September. I didn't know yet what I'd major in—probably Home Economics with some art classes too, maybe a writing class. I'd always wanted to write. The prospect of college life was a little scary—would I be accepted as a divorced mother? I was twenty years old, not too old to make new friends. I'd already made some at the Presbyterian Church we'd joined. I'd make more, I promised myself.

Life was, like the song promised, "A Bowl of Cherries" in that summer of 1941. Little did we dream of the terrible times ahead for our country and the changes they would bring to our family.

CLAIRE DE LUNE

I still catch my breath when I hear Debussy's *Claire de Lune*, even though it's been sixty years or more since I first became aware of its haunting melody. I was twenty, a freshman at San Jose State University, and more into the music of Glenn Miller or Harry James. The Big Band sounds of those orchestras seemed to fit the turbulent times we were living in. The restless, jitterbug dances we did then reflected our inner, undirected energies.

I first met Darlene—I don't remember her last name—in my fencing class that spring of 1942. Darlene was the person who set *Claire de Lune* in my memory forever. But I'm getting ahead of my story.

Fencing's stylized aggression appealed to me. I loved the thrust and parry, the clink of metal, the awkward stance that began to feel natural as the lessons progressed. Darlene was often my partner, her brown eyes watching warily as I moved, my blue ones equally intent on her. It was the last class of the day, and we began walking home together a couple of times a week.

Darlene was a quiet, thoughtful girl, a music major. I knew she played the piano.

"The children love to listen when I practice and their mother likes them out of the way while she gets dinner," she told me. She says it's a lot of help and worth my Board and Room just to keep them amused."

"What do they like best?"

"Oh, little simple tunes, like *Old McDonald* or *She'll Be Comin' Around the Mountain*. But I play some Mozart, some Debussy—they like that too."

I can still picture Darlene's face a little, though the features are smudged like in a fading black and white photo. Dark brown shoulder length hair, cut straight but curling up at the ends. We were about the same height – 5'4" or so – and similar weight too, about 120 pounds. What I really remember is the *feel* of us walking along the elm tree shaded streets together, easy, not having to prove anything. With Darlene it didn't matter that I felt different from all the other girl students. It didn't matter that I was the divorced mother of a two-year-old daughter, Judy. It was unimportant that my dissolved marriage had been a necessity, a shame and embarrassment I never wanted to reveal. She didn't ask questions.

In fact, the comfort in our relationship lay in its containment. We shared no activity other than fencing and walking together. I knew nothing of her background, except the occasional reference to her family in Northern California. There were younger siblings and I'd gotten the idea there was a strict religiosity about her early upbringing. Maybe it was her quiet manner, her reserve that made me think that. But there was a determination under the unruffled surface that sometimes made my laughter sound too loud in my own ears; a sense of purpose that hadn't made itself known yet.

I don't know what Darlene saw in me. I was balancing roles like a juggler keeping balls in the air. Student, mother, daughter, new settler in a strange community. Our family's move from Iowa the previous summer had come just in time for a new beginning for each of us. San Jose with its then population of ninety thousand swallowed me nicely.

School was o.k. I liked the Home Economic classes I was enrolled in well enough; enjoyed History and Life Drawing and the World Lit classes too. I supposed I would end up being a Home Ec teacher like Mother had been, though the thought was not exciting. It was hard to think of teaching, marrying, leading a "normal" life when everything was turned upside down with the War: boys leaving school, headlines in the papers shouting defeat every day. Blackouts. Even my brother, Paul, leaving to work in the shipyards in Vallejo before the Draft got him: Dad's new job which had gotten us to California swallowed up by the war effort. Everything was upset.

Darlene and I talked about uncertainty.

"I don't know how to plan, what to expect. I just seem to be able to focus on one day at a time," I said. I wondered if Darlene had plans for the weekend; maybe we could go to a movie. I almost knew what her answer would be.

"I can't," she said. "I'm going somewhere." She didn't elaborate.

Well, I had a day of work at Kress's on Saturday; homework on Sunday. Judy to think about. A Saturday night at home wouldn't hurt. But there was something reserved about the way Darlene said she was "going somewhere" that drew a curtain between us. Maybe it was because she didn't smile like you do when you're anticipating a happy time.

"Are you going to be with your friend?" I asked. She'd told me about her man friend, older than she by ten years. He's twenty-nine, I thought. That's old! I wondered if he was interested in her girlish aspirations or whether she suppressed them to seem older and more sophisticated when she was with him. They seemed to spend secluded time together—no football games or dances. They loved to go to the movies, Darlene said, and told me about seeing Bette Davis in *Now Voyager*.

"He was a married man, but not happy. You should have seen the look in his eyes when he lit two cigarettes and gave her one of them!" We walked silently for a while.

Sometimes Darlene told me about nice restaurants in Palo Alto like *Dinah's Shack* or *L'Omellette* where they could linger for hours at dinner. It all sounded very romantic. But a married man! Why would she go out with a married man? I couldn't picture him at all: she could have said *Chinese* or *Persian* and I'd have had equal difficulty. He was a dark blur in my imaginings. I wondered if they slept together, but all I said was, "Do you think you'll marry him someday?"

"Oh no! That won't ever happen!" She didn't say why and the way her mouth shut in a thin line, I didn't ask again. We continued our after school walks home for the next few weeks, comfortable in each other's companionship.

One Monday, Darlene was absent from class and I briefly wondered why as I hurried home in a light spring rain. My mind was on little Judy, who'd come down with a cold the day before. There was nothing to worry about, with Mother at home to take care of her, but still my steps were quicker than usual. I'd read her a story and make some lemonade before dinner. My zippered leather binder was heavy in my left hand and I scooped the afternoon *San Jose News* with my right as I entered the front door. I could see what was becoming a too familiar headline in the paper "JAPAN ATTACKS..." in the headlines and handed the paper to Mother. I'd tend to Judy before reading it.

Monday night dinner was always the same: left over roast from Sunday's midday dinner, sliced thin with mashed potatoes and gravy. If we'd had pie on the weekend, it was gone and there was pudding for dessert. If Mother had made a cake, white with coconut frosting or our favorite Sunshine Yellow with thick icing, we'd have that with Jell-O.

While we ate, we talked. Dad had a story to tell; brother Bob an anecdote about his eighth grade science class. Finally Mother spoke. "Isn't it a shame about that young couple they found in the motel?"

"What young couple?"

"She was a student at State. I wonder if you knew her. Her name was Darlene."

Grabbing the paper from the sideboard, I sank into a chair. There was Darlene's picture staring at me. Even now, I'm uncomfortable thinking about the story I read—the story of two lovers who had ended their lives by means of a hose attached to the exhaust pipe of their car, Debussy's *Clair de Lune* playing its lovely mournful notes as they died. The phonograph was still circling aimlessly when the motel manager found their bodies, the paper said. I sat in stunned disbelief trying to understand. Nothing in my own life had ever produced such despair as Darlene must have felt.

In the weeks that followed, I wrestled with the suicide. The image of my gentle friend lying on a strange bed with her lover as she waited to die haunted me. I searched my memory for clues that might have warned me of her intent, but could think of nothing. If only I could have helped her in some way!

Only when I hear *Claire de Lune* do I feel again the spell of the music that represents to me the romantic, ironic caprice of life opening the door to tragedy when just a mirror glance away is another possibility, another history to be written.

I don't have a marker in my memory for when the first shock of Darlene's death began to wear off; when I could think of it without an inner turning away from the terrible, and final, decision she had made for herself. Even now, I feel tension, a tightening in my chest when I peer into the abyss of her death: of any self-inflicted death. It is a measure I have never contemplated for myself. And yet, there is admiration too: admiration for her sureness of purpose that transcended what must have been many doubts and fears. And anger! How could she! How could she have cast aside the love and promise of her young life! What right did she have to hurt all those who loved her, who would never understand, would spend many years grieving and pondering why she left them behind without a word? I am surprised at this surge of anger, when it has not surfaced before. I think it is because as my own years accumulate, I can realize what a precious gift life is, one not to be thrown away. And I realize too how I've come to understand actions of others that once seemed unacceptable.

Only when I hear *Clair de Lune* do I think of that sad event in my youth, and when its mournful melody begins its spell I can understand a little the romantic dark magic that swept Darlene and her lover along in its path to their deaths.

BLIND DATE

What was I doing here, sitting alone at this little round Formica topped table in a smoke-filled nightclub in Sunnyvale at nine o'clock in the evening? I wasn't even sure where Sunnyvale was; except that it was somewhere close to Moffett Field where the Army had been stationed since the War began. And where was my "blind date", that dark browed guy with the shifty eyes that never looked at me, but somewhere else in the room? I didn't even remember his name.

When Betty had called late that afternoon, and described the party arranged by some friends of hers at "State", it had sounded like fun.

"Some soldiers from Moffett Field are coming, and they want to meet girls from school. I know one of the guys and he's o.k. Come on, it'll be fun."

So I had come along with Betty for a lark. I was tired of spending my evenings studying; I needed a break, some excitement in my life. Everything was so changed since the War started, so uncertain. I'd been feeling tense, vaguely apprehensive as though the atmosphere had grown heavier as it does before a storm. I could read Judy her nightly bedtime story, help Mother with the dishes, and still be ready in time. "O.K.", I'd said. "I'll go as long as we won't be out too late." I had a class in the morning.

But here I was perched on this ridiculous ice cream parlor chair, legs crossed and hoping my skirt wasn't too short: alone with a jukebox blaring in the corner, and strangers all around me laughing and drinking from tall glasses. I tried to look cheerfully expectant, as though I was waiting for someone who was just temporarily out of the room. Betty had disappeared. How was I going to get home, and when?

"Hi," a voice interrupted my thoughts. "Can I join you?" A dark haired man moved closer into view. I noticed the uniform, the Sergeant's stripes on the sleeve. He kept talking, thrusting out his hand, "My name's Jim Cardellino. My buddies went somewhere—I saw you sitting here by yourself. I thought you might like company."

I had already noticed his trim, freshly pressed look, his smile. What harm could it do to be friendly? He seemed polite enough.

I murmured something. Anything was better than sitting here alone.

"Would you like to dance?" I always wanted to dance! Jim steered me lightly by the elbow onto the small round dance floor where two other couples were hanging onto each reminding me of those thirties dance marathons. I was relieved when Jim competently followed the beat of the jukebox music: *In the Mood, A String of Pearls and Tuxedo Junction*. Glen Miller and the Andrews sisters' music was made for dancing and it felt good to be moving to music again. Jim held me firmly, but not threateningly close. I was comfortable. I could relax.

"Let's have a drink and sit down," he said, and led me back to our table where I ordered my usual tall sweet drink, probably a Tom Collins, that I could nurse through the evening. I wasn't much of a drinker. I was a pretty good listener, though.

"Tell me about yourself," I said. "What do you do in the Army?"

"It's not really the Army," he said. "It's the Air Corps. I'm in it because I wanted to be a pilot, but I'm too old, I found out. I'm twenty-seven. I'm older than a lot of the guys—feels a little strange, like I'm their big brother or something. I'm in Supply—that's taking care of all the stuff the squadron needs, like blankets, shoes—that kind of thing.

"I know what you mean about feeling older—I'm that way too with some of my school friends. I was married before, not now, and I have this little two year old daughter, so sometimes they seem a little silly to me."

Jim hadn't flinched when I told him about Judy. I liked that.

And later, "You want me to take you home? I can probably borrow my buddy's car."

Oh, oh, I thought. Now I'll really be taking a chance. What might happen on a ride home with a man whom I'd just met: But he did seem nice, and so far very respectful. And really, what choice did I have? I still hadn't seen Betty, and there was that early morning class…

"All right. I do need to get home."

As we drove, I talked more about myself. Our family's recent move from Iowa, my studies at San Jose

State. He told me that the car he'd borrowed belonged to John Wenzel, a San Jose resident and member of his Squadron.

"They've practically adopted me, John and his brother. I've stayed at their house several times. His mom calls me Jimmy. They live just off The Alameda, so I've gotten to know San Jose a little."

Jim drove confidently, and found South Fourteenth Street easily. When we reached the front door of the house, he kissed me lightly on the cheek and said,

"Don't get married or anything before I see you again!"

After that first meeting in February, Jim was a frequent visitor, calling me for dates whenever he had a pass, taking me to nice places to eat, sometimes the Saint Claire Hotel in San Jose, or *L' Omelette* in Palo Alto, expensive and elegant. Sometimes he lit my after dinner cigarette, one of the few I smoked during the day, with his own. Very romantic, I thought. He especially endeared himself to me the first time he met Judy. Dropping to his knees to be at her level, he hugged her warmly, saying to me later,

"Mama Mia! She's so beautiful! What a little sweetheart!"

Mother and Dad liked this serious young man who was treating me so well, and I did too, though I wasn't "in love," but what did that matter in these strange wartime days when men students on campus were joining the Army or Navy by the score; when diamond engagement rings sparkled on many coeds' fingers. I wasn't surprised when, in early June, Jim asked me to marry him.

"I'm just not sure," I equivocated. "And what about

OCS? I thought you wanted to go to the Officer Candidate School like your buddies have been urging you to sign up for, and the Captain said he'd recommend you—what about that? Give me a couple of weeks to think about it,"

The Navy had taken over Moffett Field during the spring and Jim's squadron had been moved to Chico, so his visits were less frequent now. I would have a couple of weeks to think things over before his next visit.

"O.K., but I hope you'll say yes. I'm crazy about you!"

I wished I felt that way, instead of just the immense respect Jim engendered in me. Was that enough? Shouldn't I be madly in love, thinking of him day and night? Maybe I was beyond those feelings, what with my former marriage and Judy and all? But he loved Judy so much—she was already calling him "Daddy Jim"—she needed a daddy. And who knew how many young men would come back from the war, or whether the ones that did would want a woman with a child? Did it matter that Jim lacked the *joi de vivre* I had hoped for in a husband. Couldn't I be the one to furnish that in our relationship? And I didn't even know his family back in Pennsylvania, but he said they'd love me and I'd like them. I probably would.

And what about after the war? Jim had been a salesman.

"I can always get a job," he'd assured me. "And I want to adopt Judy and live in California."

I felt like a juggler, tossing arguments into the air; catching them adroitly so they never really hit ground: common sense on one side, my romantic desires on the other. Common sense won out, and on his next visit I told Jim I would marry him.

"But after you graduate from OCS, honey." I announced.

We could get married first, he said, but I demurred. No going off to Florida where it was said there was little housing. I'd stay in San Jose and wait, keep on going to school. I'd had enough changes in my life in the past couple of years.

My stubbornness was the push Jim needed to make the decision to go to Officers' Candidate School, one he would never regret, though in later years he sometimes accused me of not having loved him enough to marry him without an officer's commission.

There would be other times in the future when I would encourage Jim to take on new responsibilities, each one a turning point in his life

THE SUMMER OF '42

By the end of my freshman year at San Jose State, all students were urged to help in the war effort wherever they could. Consequently, a few weeks after school ended I did what hundreds of my classmates were doing: went to work in a cannery. In my case, it was the Del Monte plant on Auzerais Street in San Jose. The nation needed canned fruit and vegetables that summer as never before. The armed services were buying food in unprecedented quantities. Because so many men had left for the service and many people—men and women—had gone to build the Victory ships at Richmond and Vallejo, there was a shortage of labor in the local canneries. The industry had traditionally employed students during the summer months but never in such numbers as in the needy summer of 1942.

I found myself in a completely new world: a world of noisy machines, shouting voices, coarse language, harsh floor ladies ready to pounce on every error we young workers made. I was terrified of them. I wore my shoulder length hair in a net with a stiff white cap fastened on securely with bobby pins. My oldest clothes were covered with a long breast-to-ankle rubber apron; awkward rubber gloves covered my hands and wrists.

Each "canner", all women, stood in appointed spot in front of "her" sink, more the size of a laundry tub than an ordinary kitchen variety. Above the sink was a large chute, through which the golden apricots halves fell in sporadic clumps into the space below. An eye level shelf above the sink held dozens of empty glass jars. Glass was new this year, since the government had requisitioned just about every kind of metal for the first-priority weapons industry. The glass was more difficult to handle than number two tin cans and a broken jar with its treacherous slivers of glass amongst the fruit was to be avoided at all costs.

"Floor ladies" authoritarian women who had worked in the cannery for years, roamed the aisles like predatory hawks watching and waiting for mistakes.

Time meant money, for we were paid by "piece work"— so much money for each tray of a dozen jars. The Cannery Workers' Union, to which we all belonged, assured a minimum wage of thirty-three and a half cents an hour, but everyone wanted to make more than that—maybe a dollar an hour! We screamed jealously when we thought someone else had more fruit to work with than we did: the fruit arrived sporadically and in unpredictable amounts. We poked the apricots furiously into the jars, worked feverishly to lay the golden halves carefully onto the bottom in a pattern that would build easily as the jar filled in an elliptical design.

There was no time to think of the beauty of the operation, the poetry in the interlaced cooperation of the pickers, sorters, cutters, truckers and canners, to say nothing of the intricate machinery that operated the conveyor belts on which the fruit was dumped and the filled jars carried to their destination. I stood, working faster and harder and longer than I had ever done in my entire life. The floor ladies patrolled the walkways behind the canners, watching for errors—a spotted fruit, a jar not filled to the brim.

"Do it over! Throw that spotted one out! Fill up that jar." Each interruption slowed the worker's production time. Old timers near me moved their hands in double time movie motion. I tried to emulate them, but their automatic grace came from years of experience.

I worked the night shift. Always a morning person, I found it impossible to adjust to daytime dormancy. Sleeping on a cot in our basement didn't help: I still heard the footsteps of my family upstairs, a ringing telephone, and children playing in the July sunshine. The noises all conspired to keep me awake. The harder I tried to doze off, the more difficult it became. Fatigue built in layers, smothering my energy. Finally, even though I earned more working at night, I pled for a daytime shift and finally was granted one.

The days became easier then. I was assigned to the fruit cocktail belt, given a fixed wage of about sixty-five cents an hour, and the job of watching the fruit unceasingly as it slid by on a three-foot wide belt. I was to pick out any stems, defective fruit, leaves, or miscellaneous debris which would mar the perfection of a jar of fruit cocktail. At first, I was elated with the ease of the new responsibility. The pressure was off and I could relax a little.

However, my delight was short-lived. I stood four or five hours at a time, watching the same scene before my eyes, relieved only by one fifteen minute break in the mornings and afternoons. The monotony of the monochromatic color scheme (diced peaches, pears, pineapple, pale green grapes) was enlivened only by an occasional bright red maraschino cherry. I grew to love those cherries, their brightness pulling me back to sanity.

Men did the heavy work of loading fruit and jars, cleaning up, mechanical repairs and they were paid more. We women stood a few feet apart along the belt inspecting its contents as it cranked slowly before our eyes. Talk was impossible; the noise was too great. The big round clock on the wall opposite me seemed frozen—fifteen minutes took an hour to pass! I sang to myself all the songs I knew leaning heavily toward old Stephen Foster tunes, *Old Black Joe*, and *Swanee River* were favorites. I made up stories, thought about friends in Iowa where our family had lived until the previous June of 1941. I thought about Jim, trying to envision what marriage to him would be like—it all seemed unreal, hard to imagine yet. News of the war was too overwhelming to dwell on. It seemed far away as though it were happening on another planet.

Whatever my thoughts, the belt's inexorable passage continued. As the hot summer days passed, I became accustomed to the monotony. I stopped noticing that in the first few moments of a break period I walked like a drunken sailor; got used to grabbing for a faucet in the row of sliding sinks against the wall while my inner ear adjusted to outer reality. Payday was the highlight of the week, and my mother's often-repeated phrase "This too shall pass" sustained me.

Camaraderie sprang up between the college kids, often

strangers before the summer started. We spent lunch hours gossiping at the wooden tables under the grape arbor outside the building. One shocked noon hour we spoke in hushed tones of a contemporary, a girl, who had lost two fingers in a machine that morning. As the return to work whistle blew, we stretched weary backs and entered the cannery doors for the afternoon's long hours of belt watching or jar stuffing.

I hated the steamy, pungent smell of cooked fruit combined with acrid machine grease. I hated the all-pervasive noise, but more than that I hated the boredom of endless routine work. But I stuck out the season, and with a new appreciation of the variety college life offered, and bolstered by a tidy sum in my savings account, prepared to return to school.

MY WORLD WAR TWO

My daughter Joan said to me recently "Mom, I hope when you're writing about your life you'll put something in about World War II. I'd really like to know more about how it was then."

So I will put down what I remember. Since I've written about the early days of the war from Pearl Harbor on, I'll start with my life with Jim Cardellino as the wife of a second Lieutenant in the U.S. Air force.

It was May of 1943 when Jim and I moved to Alliance, Nebraska, with the rest of his squadron, three days after our wedding in Ft. Wayne, Indiana. Jim was the Supply officer for the unit and most of our friends were in similar, non-flying, categories such as Intelligence, Operations or Medical. Swollen into twice its size, from an original population of around 4,000, Alliance had little extra space for the servicemen and their families who flocked there. The best Jim and I could find was a small bedroom with adjacent bath just off the dining room of a one-story house on the tree lined main street We squeezed in a small cot in the corner for three-year-old Judy. There were no cooking facilities and I remember the wonderful big oatmeal cookies I bought from the German bakery for Judy's and my breakfasts after Jim had left early for the "post".

Dinners were eaten out, most frequently at the air base, and were usually a thick steak or chops of wonderful Midwest corn fed beef or pork. They were festive occasions, eaten at long wooden tables, where we laughed as though there were no cares in the world, hiding for a moment the reason we were together here in this place. We sang the Air Force songs—

Happy is the day when the Air Force gets its pay
and we are rolling, rolling home…

When we finally managed to secure another apartment on the top floor of a two-story house, I was delighted. There was a tiny kitchen where I could cook more nutritious meals for Judy and me and real dinners in the evening for Jim as well. The fact that the bathroom was down two flights of stairs did not deter us, though it was to cause real discomfort for me when I had a weeklong case of diarrhea during the summer!

Nebraska was a good place for the squadron to sharpen its skills. Located in the middle of the country, with untrammeled airspace to maneuver in, the pilots had an ideal place to fly. But after a few months, an order came that the squadron must move to another location, Lumberton, North Carolina. We wives were never told anything except what the next move would be, and I didn't want to know much more. In the back of everyone's mind was the sure knowledge that each step brought the men closer to being transferred overseas.

So in August of 1943, we left Alliance for yet another adventure—at least that is how I tried to think of it—in the Deep South But first we would stop in Blairsville, Pennsylvania where Jim's family lived.

I had never met the family before. Four were living at home now: "Pap" Jim's father, his brother Bob, disqualified for service in the Army because of a vague "nervous condition", and two sisters, Teresa and Jovina, who spent a lot of time singing to and with a giggling Judy—*"On the Good Ship Lollipop"* or *"Oh Daddy, oh Daddy, How You Can Love."* with Jovina's expressive rolling of eyes and delight on Judy's part.

I had another view of Jim on that visit, which disturbed me. I heard him, the older brother, sharply chastising Jovina for buying the wrong length shoelaces for him when she went to the store.

"Dummy—you got it wrong! Go back and get the right length!" he said angrily. It doesn't sound like much now, but the tone and demeanor shocked me. Was this the man I'd married? I couldn't imagine speaking to one of my brothers in that tone.

We had only a few days to spend with the family and left again via train, for Washington, D.C. to do a little sightseeing. Jim had spent time there in summer camps as a youth and was eager to show me some of the city.

It was hot and muggy in Washington, and the two memories that linger in my mind are of a uniformed Jim hopping off the train with Judy and one of her dolls in his arms, and of climbing all the steps to the top of the Lincoln Memorial in that muggy heat, only to have Judy announce, "I have to go wee-wee mommy."

The restrooms were at the bottom of that long flight of stairs.

So here we were in the Deep South, and it was just what I'd pictured from reading *Gone With the Wind*. Tree lined streets, white-pillared churches and houses, a small downtown area. Perfect! I thought as I fanned my face vigorously in a vain attempt to keep cool.

This time our apartment was on the top floor of a small church on the outskirts of town. There were stairs to climb again, but we did have our own bathroom—and neighbors, a couple who had lived there for years. I loved having a woman next door who could share a cup of coffee or tell me about local customs.

The first time I needed a babysitter for Judy, I asked Shirley to recommend someone.

"Get Lavonne," she said. "She's very reliable. She's good in emergencies too—the best black girl I've ever found to help out."

I took Shirley's recommendation, but not without some hesitation. I look back on that doubting now and find it strange, but in 1943 my own limitations in dealing with or knowing anything about Negroes was huge. I found the large number of blacks on the streets quite intimidating, since I'd never encountered any in such close proximity. I remember feeling uneasy when walking with Jim down the street on a hot humid summer evening in Lumberton surrounded by their strange dark bodies.

"It's o.k. Don't worry," Jim reassured me.

He was right—there were never any untoward incidents, but you must remember this was before the Civil rights movement. Jim Crow laws, which placed severe restrictions on the Negroes, like having to sit in the balcony in movie theaters, or use different drinking fountains, were still in effect. Those restrictions and many others gave the subliminal message that there was something inherently dangerous about our dark skinned citizens.

Life in Lumberton comes back to me in snippets of memory.

Heat: unbearably hot and sticky during the day in August and early September, especially on the top floor of an un-insulated, non-air-conditioned clapboard church.

Bugs: cockroaches sometimes an inch or two long in the bathtub, bugs circling the lamp in the living room at night. Long evenings, when we ran out of conversation, afraid to broach the subject of war, of separation. When we were with our friends, it was easier to be lighthearted. Part of marriage, I was to discover, was the boredom that sometimes went with it.

Jim's face, at the bottom of the stairs, as he held up a bouquet of roses he'd brought me in celebration,

"I got my promotion! I'm a First Lieutenant now!"

My own quickly concealed dismay that he'd spent extra money on flowers.

"That's wonderful, honey!"

There were unexpected pleasures. Getting up early in the morning while it was still cool, and taking a sleepy Judy with me to the Farmer's Market where the freshest eggs and vegetables were sold.

I loved talking to the townsfolk as I shopped, asking about new and unfamiliar produce.

"How do you cook these?" I queried, picking up a dull green pod of okra. "I've never eaten them."

"Oh, honey, you 'jes put 'em in a little water and steam 'em. Throw some butter in the pan too. Only takes about ten minutes, they're so fresh. I just picked 'em this mornin'"

I bought fresh brown eggs, black-eyed peas, plump tomatoes and garden lettuce, handing Judy the bag of lettuce to carry my arms were so full.

"C'mon, honey," I told her. "We'll stop at the Bakery on the way home and get a cinnamon roll for breakfast."

Going to church on a Sunday. People dressed in their Sunday best, singing hymns together, greeting one another afterward. I loved the feeling of being part of a community, however transitory it was. Walking the streets of Lumberton was different and yet somehow the same as Denison had been: white houses, deep lawns, tree-lined streets, muggy hot summer days and nights.

Once I went to a tobacco auction, stepping quietly into the barn where it was held. I was astonished at the rapidity of the auctioneer's words. How did anyone know when to bid? Occasionally I saw a hand raised in the audience of overalled farmers, but the movement was so slight I couldn't be sure if it was to brush a fly away, or dab at a trickle of sweat or an honest-to-God bid. The tobacco smelled delicious, just as I thought it should.

I found a friend, Louise Luria. Mort, her husband, was a new Second Lieutenant. with the squadron and the four of us hit it off immediately. The first time the Luria's came to visit they were laden with presents for Judy. It was like Christmas for her and their generosity of course endeared them to us. Louise and I talked endlessly and intimately about our lives, the future, and our fears. We found small shops in the town to explore, including restaurants offering delicious lunches for us to linger over.

Jim and I lying in bed after Judy was asleep talking about whether we should have a baby. "I don't want to have a child when you aren't here to be with me," I said, and the matter was settled. Jim was willing to wait.

Lonesome. I missed my family, especially my mother. I missed the kind of life we'd had together, the easy repartee, the way Mother and I smiled at one another when we made the beds or did the dinner dishes together. I missed Dad's stories and Bob's clowning around. I was twenty-two years old and I was homesick!

"You can go back home if you want to," Jim said, but I would have none of that. What kind of a wife would I be to leave a spouse when he was about to go off to war?

Emotionally, we all suffered. When we got together with friends, we drank a lot, usually beer or mixed drinks of some kind. Wine had yet to come into its own and bourbon highballs were easy to mix on a moment's notice. I remember John Kearny, former publisher of the *TRENTON TIMES* who was now the squadron Intelligence Officer, getting so drunk he couldn't get up from the floor, while his patient and understanding wife, Bobby, tried to pull him to his feet. Jim loved to drink, and was accused of having a "hollow leg" because he never seemed inebriated. I liked it too, though my usual style was to nurse a tall one for an hour or so. But liquor helped the underlying questions fade away. When would the men have to leave? What would I do while Jim was away? Why did I dread his going so little and hate the suspense more? I wondered if the other wives felt the same.

The day finally came in early December when the squadron got its orders to move in preparation to going overseas. We wives knew no details, other than the date we were to prepare to leave: no destination for the men, no idea where they would be, though rumors flew among us like panicked quail rising suddenly into the air—Europe, Africa, Italy, probably not the Pacific. The long-dreaded tearful goodbyes were said. The waiting had begun.

It began in Blairsville. I don't have a clear memory of why I went there to spend the first weeks of separation: I was desperate to get back to California and my family. My guess is that it was the only place I *could* go because of the enormous difficulty in traveling by train during wartime. Remember, there were no airlines then, no planes at all for civilian use. Trains and busses were the only means of public transportation.

Wait. That was all I could do. Wait for the weeks to pass when I would be notified I'd gotten a reserved seat on a train bound for San Jose.

"Probably won't be till after Christmas, ma'am. There's so many of the soldiers wanting to get home for the holidays."

I resigned myself to spending the holidays with Jim's family instead of my own but that resignation did not come easily. It was bitter cold. Snow blanketed the town. I was cooped up in the house with Jim's two sisters, his father and brother Robert. Two other brothers were in the Army, stationed in California. Jim was the only sibling to have married, and the others were a close knit family whose chief joy, it seemed to me, was to criticize one another and the world at large.

I took long walks on the snow-encrusted sidewalks, hoping to pass the hours, while Judy napped or played with her aunties. She was the common denominator between us, for I found I had little in common with Jim's sisters. They probably felt the same about me.

His father, though, was a sweet and gentle man whom I liked but whose English was poor (he'd come to America from Italy at the age of fourteen) and our communication was stilted. I was lonely and bored. Would this waiting never end? I felt imprisoned by the gloomy atmosphere, the snow and cold. Of course there was no word from Jim, nor did I expect to hear where he was stationed just yet. It was a time of rude awakening for me. Listening to Jovina and Teresa, Jim's sisters, bicker; hearing Jovina talk rudely to her father made me cringe and I wanted to shake her. She was my age, but I felt she sometimes acted like a fifteen year old. I didn't know then, in my own immaturity, that Jovina would show unexpected strengths when she had her own battles to fight, that we would in time become friends. Teresa, the elder, had a sweeter nature, but smiles did not come easily to her either. Bob, Jim's brother, delighted in telling me stories of Jim's shortcomings.

Finally there was news. I would be able to leave a few days after Christmas! With a definite date set, I could shake off my gloom and get into the holiday spirit. I threw myself into buying presents for everyone, finding toys for

Judy that would fit into a suitcase. We decorated a tree.

"It's the first tree we've put up since the war started," Jovina said as she helped Judy hang the red and gold balls on its branches. "It just didn't seem like Christmas with everybody gone..."

Teresa and I baked Italian Christmas cookies; Jovina sang carols with Judy. Grandpa got up early on Christmas day to make his special spaghetti sauce. Even Bob went around with a smile on his face. I was happy: I was going home in a few days!

And then, the day after Christmas, Judy showed me some spots on her tummy.

"I don't feel so good, Mommy."

Chickenpox. That's what the doctor said when he came to the house. "She'll have to be quarantined for three weeks"

Three weeks! Another delay! My heart sank. How could I endure another three weeks? I cancelled the train reservations and asked for another, later.

The time did pass. The necessary tasks of nursing Judy helped. She was not alarmingly ill, only contagious until the scabs disappeared. Reading her stories and playing games made the hours go faster. I spent a weekend in Pittsburgh with Louise Luria, a welcome respite akin to going from night to day in terms of talk and fun. I returned to Blairsville renewed, resolved to think only kindly thoughts.

We got up early on the day our train was to leave. Teresa, Jovina, Judy and I with Bob at the wheel of the car, left the house at seven to drive the forty miles to Pittsburgh to catch the ten o'clock train.

"If it's on time," Bob warned. "These trains are often late."

I'd rather stand and wait than miss it, I thought. And that is what we did, among the crowds, mostly khaki clad servicemen and their families, waiting there at the Union Pacific station. Our two suitcases at my feet, Judy in my arms, I listened anxiously for the train's whistle and to the talk swirling around me.

"You have to run like hell to get on the train," someone said. "Even if you have a reserved seat, it's tough."

Could I make it carrying Judy? What about my suitcases? I had to get on that train! I flexed my ankles. The train's whistle could be heard in the distance, at last. The crowd surged forward in anticipation as the engine appeared around the bend of track and the train stopped.

"Run, Juliana, run," Bob yelled. "I've got your suitcases." Teresa and Jovina were shouting goodbyes and I suddenly felt a surge of love for them. I ran as fast as I could, my heart thumping. Someone's hand grabbed my elbow helping propel me up the steps.

"You're on!" Bob shouted. I sank into the nearest seat, Judy on my lap, and began to laugh.

I don't remember much about that trip home, except that Judy was the darling of all the young soldiers on the train. How and where we slept and ate has gone into the mists of memory.

BREAKFAST EGGS

"Do you want an egg this morning, honey?" I asked Jim as he sat at the kitchen table in my parent's home in San Jose. It was the first meal I would cook for him since he'd returned from France a few days ago. It was May of 1945. We'd slept late that morning, indulging in some early morning lovemaking while Judy was in Sunday school where Dad had taken her.

I liked looking at Jim, his trim waist, his shiny black hair, and his clean shave. He was more rested than he'd been a few days ago when I'd met him at Mather Field in Sacramento after his long trip home, first on a troop ship, then a plane from New York. Lurking in the back of my mind were other issues we'd have to deal with soon, but this morning was mellow, full of the warmth of the eleven o'clock May sunshine, the tender memories of homecoming.

"Yep. I'm hungry. Fry me two, sunny side up. And lots of toast and jam."

Two eggs, I thought. Nobody in our family ever ate more than one, especially now that they were so expensive. What would Mother think?

Breakfast Eggs

"Are you sure you want two?"

"Sure. I always eat two eggs now. Learned to like 'em in the Army, when we could get them. Sometimes it was rough…Once in Italy…" Jim began a story of a plethora of eggs brought by villagers when he and his fellow officers stayed at a home in Italy. "They loved us," he said. "Couldn't do enough for us after we got rid of the Nazis. I talked to all of them, and they loved that I could speak the lingo."

I plopped the eggs into the sizzling bacon fat; dropped bread in the toaster. "Tell me more," I said, wondering if Jim would want two eggs every morning.

After breakfast I asked, "Do you think we could unpack some more of your stuff after breakfast? It's a little hard moving around the bedroom with your duffel bag; and suitcase in the way."

Jim had brought presents in his suitcase for everyone: a lace-gowned, exquisite French doll for Judy—

"See what a beautiful face she has! You'll look like that someday—and have a dress so pretty too!"

Cameos from Italy for Mother and me as well as French perfumes—Chanel, Guerlein, hand tooled Italian belts for Bob and Dad, a nylon parachute.

"Don't know what we'll do with it, but look at the material!" I rolled the voluminous folds of white nylon into a ball and tucked it under our bed. There were big drawers in the walk in closet of our bedroom and plenty of space to hang his few clothes. If only Judy's small bed could have been squeezed in the closet—there was a window—we'd have had more privacy. That hadn't been possible, so she slept soundly in our bedroom, but like most five year olds, was a sound sleeper and seldom awoke during the night. We could be quiet.

In the days and weeks that followed, Jim and I dealt with the other issues I'd known we'd have to: a job for him, a car, civilian clothes, how long to live with Mother and Dad.

"Can't get a job 'till I've got a car and some clothes."

"What kind of work do you think you'll look for? Do you want to go back to school? There's the G.I. bill—"

"I'm not going to school. Forget that. I'll get a job as a salesman—I'm pretty good at that. But I'll need some decent clothes. I could get some really nice suits through my dad in Blairsville—probably get a better price on a car there too. I know a guy who'd give me a deal back home."

I could tell what was coming. Jim would want to travel to Pennsylvania, and I wasn't ready for that. I'd had enough of Blairsville two years before.

"How about we take the train back to my folks, pick up a car and drive back? That way I could see them all, have a visit."

I thought about my job as a medical assistant to the Ophthalmologist I'd worked for during the time Jim had been overseas. I'd taken several weeks off because Dr. Wilkinson had also been away, but I needed to go back to work.

"Honey, I can't. I've got to go back to work soon."

"I hate your working. Why don't you quit and go with me?"

"But we need the income!" We didn't, really. I had saved most of Jim's allotment money. We had four thousand dollars in the bank, which in those days was a considerable sum, but my early Depression experience told me *don't touch that money! It's for a house, and if you start spending, it won't last!*

"You can go without me—you could take Judy with you. You know how she loves to be with you since you came home."

Jim muttered something about my "stupid job", but finally acquiesced to the idea of taking Judy on the trip. His reservations about the inconvenience of traveling with a small girl child were assuaged when I reassured him,

"There's always someone, some woman, who will be glad to take her to the bathroom, help her brush her teeth— all that. She makes friends with everyone on a train. You'll see. And your sisters will be so happy to see Judy again. It won't be any bother."

And so they went, to be gone for two weeks. When I returned home from work in the evenings, the house seemed echoingly quiet without Judy's boisterous greeting; without Jim's deep voice talking with Dad in the kitchen while he mixed drinks for dinner. Those cocktails were something new in our family too. We'd never had drinks with dinner before, but Jim had been so persuasive, buying the liquor himself and taking such obvious pleasure in the custom, that we grownups grew to look forward to the relaxing hour before the evening meal.

Surprisingly, I found myself enjoying the time alone. There had been a lot of adjustments in the few months since the war ended. I thought about the evening in July when Jim had suddenly said at the dinner table—

"There's something I need to tell you all. I told Dedie when I first met her that I'd gone to college—to Pitt—but that wasn't true. I never went to college. I guess I just wanted to impress her. But it's been bothering me."

Mother and Dad had given hasty reassurances at this, but I sat mute and embarrassed, trying hard to swallow the bite I'd just taken that had suddenly grown to the size of a golf ball... How could Jim have lied to me? I think now that it made little difference after all, but at that time the betrayal stunned me.

Conversation, the easy flow of words I had so blithely thought I had the wit to provide, was often difficult. Jim was more given to pronouncements than discussion. There was no room for verbal exploration: a subject was either good or bad, right or wrong.

There were occasions when I wanted to talk about something besides the war, a book for instance, or a movie we'd just seen.

"What did you think of the way that picture ended? Did you think the girl should have been punished?"

"It was o.k. I guess."

Book talk was out of the question. Jim was a reader of the sports pages. His observations about politicians were apt to be,

"They're all crooked. They're just in it for the money they get on the side."

I knew from past experience that this was all I could expect, but getting used to it again took effort. I didn't always like having Jim around; he often had a negative way of looking at things that made me uncomfortable, perhaps because they flew in the face of my idealistic views of the world. That we weren't "soul mates" I had known before, but sometimes his lack of response to the humorous side of life left me feeling bereft. It got better after a few drinks in the evening, I'd noticed.

Yes, this quiet time was good. I was glad to be back at work, making appointments, putting drops in patients' eyes, taking dictation for long letters to the Mayo Clinic. I enjoyed the professional relationship with Dr. Wilkinson, even tolerated his excruciating emphasis on detail, particularly in regard to patient communication. In the early days of my employment, it was not unusual for him to dart out of an exam room, where I thought his attention was fully occupied, to say something like: "It's better to say 'May I have your name', rather than 'Can I have your name' when you're talking with patients, Juliana."

And another time, "I'll probably never tell you when you're doing things right, but I will correct you if they're wrong."

That early training was over by now, and I took pride in my professional demeanor and the ease with which we worked together. It was true I'd had some fantasies about an affair with the handsome bachelor doctor during those war years, but that was natural wasn't it? I'd have been scared to death if anything had come of them, a suggestive remark or an off color joke. But that hadn't happened. Jim was jealous, I knew, but without reason. I wanted to keep on with this job I loved.

The two weeks passed quickly and before I knew it, Jim was back, driving a new, very dusty, Plymouth sedan.

"Got a good deal on it," he said proudly as I examined the interior, and Judy clamored for attention,

"Every time Daddy got hungry, I peeled a banana for him, or gave him a cracker or a coke. We had lots of hamburgers on the way home! We sang songs—it was so much fun!" I could see that the trip had been a bonding experience for both of them, and I was glad. Glad too, that Jim's adoption of Judy had gone through so quickly a month ago.

A few days later, a large box was delivered: the tailor made suits Jim's father had ordered for him had arrived. We opened the box carefully, examining the dark worsted charcoal gray, the lighter blue gabardine, two pairs of slacks in light and dark brown.

"Look at this material!" Jim said, already trying on a jacket. "The fit's perfect."

I nodded, thinking privately that I still preferred the handsome uniform with the Captain's bars he'd worn when he first arrived.

Jobs were not easy to come by in those first months after World War II, especially if one did not have a profession to fall back on, and Jim spent time fruitlessly looking for suitable work as a salesman. I was glad I'd kept on working, though my small salary of ninety dollars a month did little more than pay our day-to-day expenses. One evening when I returned home, Jim greeted me at the front door with a broad smile, a larger than usual hug.

"Got a job today!" he announced. "It's not much, but it's a start. I'm gonna sell women's shoes at Chandler's, downtown."

I knew the store, a small establishment nestled in among the many retail stores then on First Street in San Jose—Blum's, Appleton's, Hart's and Hales, upscale jewelry shops, Woolworth's, several men's' clothiers—all were in the busy shopping area that drew customers from all over the valley.

Jim was a good salesman, often meeting or surpassing his quota for the day and earning extra money by so doing, but even so, the pay was only average and we wanted more security. We had started to look for a house to buy, but prices seemed astronomical to us. Houses that before the war had sold for half as much, now commanded eight or nine thousand dollars, sometimes more. We would have to go into debt to buy one, a thought that repelled both of us with our memories of the Depression still fresh.

"What's your hurry?" Dad said. "You can stay here till you find the right place."

Jim had finally convinced me to stop working in August, and by September I was pregnant. Surely by the time the baby came, we'd have our own home, I thought. But something was wrong with this pregnancy—there were numerous trips to the doctor for injections to control unexplained bleeding. I felt uneasy and scared, unsure of my body, as though I'd lost control of it. Mother's worried expression didn't help, though she tried to stay cheerful.

"You'll be fine, honey," she reassured me. "It's just your body getting used to things."

But on Halloween night, while Judy pranced around in her witch's costume, anxious to go trick or treating, I began to bleed heavily. I was shaking uncontrollably

"You take her out, honey," I said to Jim. "I'll stay here in bed. Mother will be here with me." He brought me the bedpan before he left, and took Judy by the hand.

Somehow, the loss did not upset me a great deal. When my doctor assured me, "You'll have other children. Sometimes Nature casts off a defective fetus, so perhaps it's for the best. Try to look at it that way." I believed him

I found another position with a surgeon, Dr. Zanger, an older man whom Jim did not object to, and whose nurse, Angie, took a motherly interest in showing me how to do things.

But underneath was a feeling of waiting, of time lost. I wanted my own home, my own "real life" to begin. I wondered when it would be time to make decisions for the future.

I BUILT A BIRDHOUSE ONCE

One night at the dinner table, over pie and coffee, Dad said,

"Why don't you build your own house, Jim? I built a garage in Sioux City once. It wasn't so hard."

I gulped, remembering that garage with its dirt floor and dim interior where I had once persuaded several neighborhood kids to defecate onto its dusty surface so I could watch the process. Surely building a garage was no guarantee that one could build a house!

"I dunno. I built a birdhouse once, but that's it. Never had any experience building."

Dad kept on talking about people who could help, following blueprints, doing your own contracting, while my mind stubbornly shut the door on each proposal. How could Jim do that, when he had no experience and was working full time?

It was true that we now had a piece of property to build on, thanks to a new subdivision called "Valley Homes" between Campbell and Los Gatos. A group of veterans had banded together to buy forty acres in an old prune orchard, where they'd partitioned off eighty home sites and a two-acre park playground. We'd met a number of our future neighbors, all young veterans eager to move into new homes and start their families. Some, like us, already had children. It was going to be a good place to live, but building our own house was a radical idea! I was sure the best plan was to have the contractor who was putting up most of the houses build ours as well.

Jim, however, was not so sure.

"You know, I could probably do it," he said a few days later.

"Do what?"

"Build our house. Valley Homes already has an architect, Gifford Sobey. We could tell him what we want, and he'd have all the specifications in the plan.

And I could get Chuck Caruthers—hire him to work with me. He's a master carpenter, not just an ordinary one. I could quit my job and work full time on the house..."

"But you've never done anything like it before!"

"I can learn. Steve Anderson and Ellis Rother and Bob Ueltzen are building their own places. We'll all help each other."

The plan was making more sense to me as he talked. Jim's enthusiasm was contagious. I could keep on working for our day-to-day expenses, and we could stay on with Mother and Dad. We all got along so well together.

We had enough cash to get the building started, maybe to complete it with the money we'd save by building ourselves. We scoured magazines—*Sunset, Better Homes and Gardens, House Beautiful*, for house plans, finally finding one that suited us perfectly: three bedrooms, two baths, large living room with a picture window looking South onto the garden, a sunny kitchen with the morning sun pouring in. I could envision it all: me in a clean housedress making coffee in the mornings before Jim went to work, the children playing quietly together.

From the architect's newly drawn plans, Jim built a dollhouse for Judy to scale, "just for practice" he said. I bought dollhouse furniture and took delight in arranging it, just as I had when my father had made a dollhouse for me when I was ten.

The exterior of our home would be redwood; some of the interior would be wood paneling. We wanted the rustic, natural look that was popular then. I had read "The Fountainhead", and was full of ideas about integrity of design. Our home would be perfect, a magnificent 1400 square feet!

One warm June day, as we surveyed the lot still filled with the old prune trees standing like some ancient guardians of the past with their gnarled limbs now sprouting meager fresh green leaves, Jim decided to clear the space where the house would be.

"Watch this," he said, and began running around the orchard, strong-arming the trees like a football tackler, while Judy clapped her hands over her mouth in glee and I watched in amazement. The selected trees gave way easily, trunks cracking, branches lying loose on the ground. "C'mon" he said, " you can drag them into a pile in the back."

The space we needed stood empty, ready to be filled with the house. We were on our way!

Jim was in his element; dealing with lumberyards for building materials, finding the best center cut redwood siding for the exterior, the cheapest plumber he could locate to install the copper tubing pipes we wanted. He worked alongside Chuck Caruthers, learning basic carpentering skills, made arrangements for needed inspections, arranged for another new homemaker, a professional electrician, to install the wiring when the time came.

When the time came—there was the rub. It seemed to me every task took eons to complete. We were always waiting for some key action to take place before the next step could be taken. We waited for the foundation to be dug, the forms built, and the inspectors to come and approve it all. Then we waited for what seemed endless days for the busy cement contractor to get around to pouring cement. Sometimes it was just a wait for the last cup of coffee to be downed by the volunteer helper of the day. Even with Jim devoting all his time to the project, it seemed painfully slow. But, bit-by-bit, each stage of the construction did happen.

Judy and I walked through the stud-framed rooms, planning together. "Look Mommy, this is MY bedroom!" while I mentally furnished the living room with a couch and chairs. I knew what would be in the dining room. We had bought a round oak table and six chairs, as well as a few other pieces of furniture, from a retiring dentist and his wife who were moving to a smaller home. The table had enough leaves to stretch out to seat as many as eighteen people, and we were to use it for many years. It is still in my home today, along with a Birdseye maple chest of drawers purchased at the same time.

We were getting to know our neighbors. Two of the families, one next door, the other across the street, had moved into their garages while their homes were under construction. The men exchanged labor, helping each other put up sheetrock, nail shingles onto roofs, lay pipe for radiant heating.

Often there were potluck suppers on warm evenings, when Steve Anderson played his guitar and we all sang *Home on the Range, She'll be Comin' Around the Mountain, Old MacDonald Had a Farm.* It was surprising how many people could fit into a garage to prepare and eat a meal!

By the spring of 1948, the house was really taking shape. The roof was almost completely shingled, the redwood siding nailed in place. We would be able to move into a partially completed house by fall.

In June, Jim began a new job with the San Jose Ice Company, selling ice refrigeration for vegetables to grocery stores, and iceboxes to homeowners. With his usual enthusiasm, he convinced me that an icebox was far superior to electric refrigerators for optimum food preservation. Some of our neighbors were persuaded as well. About half a dozen families would have new iceboxes in their just-finished kitchens, along with their automatic dishwashers and new stoves.

I was pregnant again, this time without problems, expecting a baby in October. I quit my position with Dr. Zanger in June and helped whenever I could in the final stages of preparation for moving into our partially finished house, taking particular pride in staining the kitchen cabinets in a natural wood finish. We would have two completed bedrooms; a kitchen and a half-bath nestled in to the shell of still bare studs in the rest of the house.

By late August we had moved our few possessions

into our new abode. Judy started school, and I settled back to wait for the baby to arrive. Our real life had finally begun!

THE UNINVITED GUEST

Bob Cardellino had arrived a few days after Thanksgiving, and I was trying hard to be magnanimous about it. I didn't like Jim's brother, never had from the moment I met him a tall, thin, long faced man with blue eyes, thinning hair and the longest fingers I'd ever seen: A wraith-like man who always seemed to be on the fringes of life. He had come without notice, calling from the bus station for Jim to pick him up.

"I thought I'd come out and spend the winter with you guys, now that you're in your new home and all." he'd told Jim on the phone.

He'd made the trip from Blairsville, Pennsylvania by bus, a three day trip, sleeping on the bus, eating God knew what. I had yet to find out why he was with us, except to surmise he didn't want to spend another cold Pennsylvania winter at home, where he lived with his two sisters, his father and now two older brothers who had returned from their service in the Army. Jim was the only sibling in the Cardellino family to have married. Not only had he acquired a wife five years ago but a now eight-year-old daughter, Judy, as well as a six-week-old infant son, James

Paul, named for his two grandfathers.

And now, here was Bob in our home, lurking like a shadow in the huge unfinished living room where we'd set up a cot for him. We had our new house all right, but it was a shell of what it would be when finished. *There is still so much to do! Having Bob here will slow us down even more. It isn't fair!* I tried to put a good face on the situation but my resentment seethed underneath.

Jim was doing quite well as a salesman, but even at that, our income was tight with two children and all the things still needed for the house…And now, an extra mouth to feed! I knew that was a petty form of resentment, and couldn't help myself. It wasn't the extra effort—what did it take to add a few more potatoes and carrots to a stew or make a little more hot cereal in the morning—it was the diversion of Jim's time and energy when he had so much to do in order to finish the house. And I hated not being just our own family for the first time in years, even though the time spent at my parent's home had been very pleasant. I felt cheated of this special time in our lives.

"What are your plans, Bob?" I asked one day as he lolled about the kitchen while I made a pie.

"Oh, I don't know. Maybe I'll get a job."

That would be great, I thought. Give him something to do and he wouldn't be hanging around all day.

"You know about men's clothing," I said. Bob had worked with his father in the family tailoring business in Blairsville. Though he was the only sibling to have had a college education, and had for a brief time taught music in a public school, even had a girlfriend, he was now largely dysfunctional due to a "Nervous breakdown" for which he'd received electric shock treatments. He had a mixed status in the family—looked up to for his higher education, yet babied for his nervous temperament. They made excuses for Bob. He reminded me of a white moth fluttering helplessly outside a lighted window.

"I bet you could get a Christmas job selling men's clothing at one of the department stores in San Jose," I said.

"Maybe. Yeah, I could try."

"Jim could take you into town on his way to work and you could apply at Hart's or Hales."

The seed I'd planted had taken root: Bob had gotten a job for the holidays. He sold men's socks and ties at Hales department store, even taking the bus into town when his hours were inconvenient for Jim to take him. I began to relax, thinking this might work out, after all. I'd love to see Bob get work and be independent. It would be good for him. My sanguine mood persisted as I busied myself preparing for the holidays, nursing Jimmy, helping Judy make Christmas presents, baking cookies and planning for our first tree. Even though our living room had only bare studs on the walls and a plywood floor waiting for its final hardwood cover, the fireplace was cozy and the southern winter sun streamed cheerily through huge picture windows during the day. A tree would be festive, add light and color. We had lots to celebrate!

A day or two before Christmas, Bob showed me some things he'd gotten for Jim,

"Got him some nice ties and handkerchiefs. Some good socks too—look, at these shirts," he said. He has good taste, I thought. It's really thoughtful of him.

"Gosh, Bob—even with a discount, these things

must've cost you a lot," I said.

"Didn't cost me anything," he said with a conspiratorial look. "I've been getting them for a couple of weeks now. Nobody pays any attention if you just take a little at a time..."

My heart sank. *They'll find out at the store! What a crummy thing to do! It would serve him right if he got fired.* But I only said I don't think you should have done that, and didn't tell Jim. After all, the thing was done.

And sure enough, on Christmas eve, Bob got his notice that his services would no longer be required, not unexpected since he'd been hired only as temporary help. I never brought up the subject of the procurement of Jim's gifts when he opened them the next day.

January, with its long stretches of rainy days and cold weather, kept Bob and me indoors together. Sometimes he'd help me with small chores; sometimes he spent hours walking about the neighborhood or talking to my backyard neighbor I *hope he isn't telling Margaret all his troubles, I thought.*

One day, after a particularly lugubrious conversation, I suggested to Bob that he might like to see a Psychologist.

"Yeah, I could do that, but they generally don't know much," he replied. Encouraged, I made an appointment for him with someone at the County Mental Health department. And he did go a time or two while I talked optimistically to myself about the possible positive outcome this could bring. *If only he could get a handle on his problems and take charge of his life! He has a lot of potential.*

But such was not to be. After a few sessions, Bob announced one day,

---

"I'm not going back there any more. That doctor doesn't know anything. He's no help to me." My heart sank, but I accepted that there was nothing I could do. *I'd better quit playing God and take care of my own problems,* I thought.

As the winter months wore on, Bob and Jim spent increasing hours together in the evenings and on weekends, usually in conversations stressing Bob's troubles in life, his inability to cope, what his future held. I heard bits and pieces of conversation as I busied myself with household chores, Judy's homework, and the care of a now four-month-old baby. The novelty of living in an unfinished house had worn off, and I was anxious for the work to be finished. Some things did get done: tile was laid in the large bathroom, sheetrock went up in the third bedroom. I could see that Jim was under pressure, feeling responsible for his brother's well being, yet unable to advise him in a way that Bob would accept. I often overheard conversations about the strange interdependence of the family back in Blairsville.

"You were the only one to get out, Jase...You were lucky. We all should have..."

Another time, "If only Pap had kicked us all out when we were young! We'd be better off..." I thought to myself, it's not your Dad's fault. You should have stayed in teaching. It was difficult for me to see where Dad Cardellino had failed. After his wife's death when the youngest child was born, he had provided for his family of six the best way he could, sending several of the children to live with his mother-in-law and keeping house with the three older boys himself. He supported the family by giving music lessons, leading the town band, and operating his own tailoring shop on the main street of the small town. Who was to blame him if his sons Tom and John and eventually Robert, chose to help him in the store? Wasn't it a natural thing for Teresa and Jovina to live at home and keep house for the family? Why should he "kick them out"? They would find their own way soon enough. But soon enough never arrived, except in Jim's case, and the family had settled into a routine.

I tried talking to Jim about the situation. "What are you going to do?" I asked. He shrugged and held out his hands palms up. "I dunno. What can I do? He's my brother. Don't bug me." I could see there was no conversation possible on this issue and my own frustration grew. Didn't I have some rights here? I tried to see the humorous side of the situation, but it eluded me. *I'll laugh at some of this later,* I thought *but it sure isn't funny now.*

Jim was showing visible signs of strain, with pressure from his work, the demands of the house and worry about Bob. He grew impatient with Judy (was Bob spreading tales about her to Jim, I wondered), silent and morose around me.

One evening, just before bedtime, I came into the small bathroom unexpectedly and found Jim standing before the sink, weeping, his shoulders shaking with emotion.

"What's the matter, honey? Are you hurt?"

"No. It's Bob. I just don't know what to do about him...I can't seem to help him..."

Rage engulfed me, along with a fierce protectiveness I hadn't known I possessed. No one should be doing this to our family!

"Don't worry. I'll tell Bob in the morning he has to leave. We've done all we could for him: he's got to learn to help himself. He can go back to Blairsville. I'll make arrangements in the morning. I'll take care of everything and you can blame it all on me."

I could see Jim relax. "O.K.", he said, his shoulders still in a dejected slump. For the first time since Bob had arrived, I felt strong and in control.

Two days later, I stood on the front porch with Jimmy in my arms, saying goodbye to Bob. "You'll be fine," I said. "It will be good for you to be back with the family in Blairsville."

I watched as Jim and Bob pulled out of the driveway and turned to go back into the house. Already a sense of relief and lightness engulfed me, and I stepped into our sunny living room with a renewed feeling of confidence. It had been a bad time, but I'd been equal to it. Now we could get on with our lives!

Chickenhearted

I often wished my firstborn daughter had not learned to read so well. It wasn't that Judy spent so much time with books—if she had been content to curl up in a corner somewhere, lost in a world of Kings and Queens, fairies and dragons, emerging dreamy-eyed but unthreatening—I could have understood. But Judy transposed the written word into our daily lives in ways that changed them: in beginnings that always started innocuously, gathering momentum like the proverbial rolling stone which inevitably found me in its path.

The first event that I remember happened shortly after my husband Jim and I had moved into a new semi-rural neighborhood where Judy at age nine was the oldest child on a street filled with growing families. It was shortly after World War Two and the injunction to multiply was a silent drumbeat filling cribs all over the nation. Her closest playmates were several years younger and the teacher gene, so strong in female members of our family, showed its first evidence in my daughter.

One day she read an item in the newspaper about a need for tap-dance instructors. How Judy made any connection to herself as a dance teacher stretches the imagination, for her experience with tap-dancing was not a stellar one. True, she had taken lessons for a grueling year when she was four going on five, a year when home practice sessions often ended in tears from her and angry mutterings from me. That was the year I learned I wasn't the all-patient mother I aspired to be and found the childrearing books didn't help when a stubborn mother-daughter pair locked horns.

"Hop, Step, *Shuffle*, Ball Change," I would shout after the fourth shuffle attempt had ended on the wrong foot and the tempo irretrievably lost. "Don't forget the Ball Change! Let's do it again..." as I moved the needle back to the beginning of "Peg O'My Heart". I watched Judy's fellow dancers during class time, hoping for a mother's blindness to imperfection, but seeing all too well that she did not quite keep up with the others.

Nevertheless, Judy was in the recital, wearing a costume I'd made from slippery orange satin with a hand-sewn lace trim. Her stage presence was confident as she smiled broadly at the audience while happily tapping out of sync to the music. I took lots of snapshots to send to her Daddy overseas. After all, he wouldn't know if she kept time or not!

All of which had no dampening effect on Judy's enthusiasm for starting a dance class of her own in our garage. I watched her crayoning signs to take around the neighborhood and told myself no mother would send her child to a dance class taught by a nine year old—especially one with so little training as Judy. I put the idea out of my mind and hoped she wouldn't be too disappointed if no pupils showed up.

A few weeks later, as I sprinkled clothes on the kitchen table in preparation for ironing, the unmistakable tinny sound of shoe taps emanated from our garage. Peering through a crack in the door, I was astonished to find all the children in the neighborhood who could walk, about a dozen in number, gazing raptly up at Judy's earnest, freckled face. She was demonstrating the shuffle step to them, her skinny feet and legs executing it perfectly. The age range of pupils was wide, from seven-year-old Diane to fifteen-month-old Pamela, who stood tentatively shifting her weight from side to side.

The class met regularly for several weeks, with Judy marshalling her students onto benches she'd made from planks balanced on bricks, where the children sat still and silent while she demonstrated the steps. A chance conversation with one of the mothers enlightened me as to the reason for the parental cooperation.

"Are you kidding? An hour's worth of babysitting for the fifteen cents she charges for the class? That's a real bargain, and my kids love it! They'll do anything Judy tells them to!"

I was to remember that quote many times.

A year or so later, Judy read a story about a carnival and became so entranced with the idea of being a part of such a glamorous world that she decided to create one for herself.

"Just think, Mommy! We could have it in the park on the 4th of July!" The park was a two-acre communally owned portion of land at the end of our street. It was equipped with half a dozen swings, a huge cement slab, the use for which had not yet been devised, and multitudinous weeds. It could stand some use.

"Well, all right. If you can get the other children to help you."

My words were like the smell of smoke to a fire horse, as my father used to say. Judy spent the entire winter making up "acts" for the Carnival, persuading her friends to take part as clowns, trapeze artists, "ducking heads" for ball throwing contests. She solicited promises for candy, cookies and soft drink donations. Busy as I was with young Jimmy and baby Cathy, I was glad for any activity that kept her energies happily and productively occupied. The project would wear itself out soon enough, I told myself.

Judy had a lot of sore throats that winter. I didn't notice for a while that the onset was usually on a Monday morning, often after a weekend of carnival planning with her friends. I was glad she convalesced rapidly while busily cutting and gluing favors in her bed, humming to herself as the pile of scrap paper on the floor pyramided. It didn't dawn on me until the third time I wrote an absence excuse on a Tuesday morning that a suspicious pattern had developed. Enough of that! I thought as I signed my name and consoled myself with the thought that Judy's creativity may have been more productive than a day at school, where she was head of her class.

The carnival gained in momentum all spring, though not without its troubles.

"Mommy, Debby won't do it!" Judy tearfully announced one day.

"Won't do what?"

"She won't be the Ducking Head!. She says Pammy has

to do it too, and her head's too small! No one'll be able to hit her with the balls and they won't play! It's going to ruin everything if Debby won't."

"Well, what d'you think you can do about it? Is there someone bigger?"

"I know—I'll ask Phil! Maybe he and Tommy can take turns. Debby can help me at the Koolaid stand."

The carnival was hugely successful. Judy seemed everywhere at once, giving orders, announcing events, and gleefully counting money at day's end. And as I could have predicted, I was deep in cookie dough and lemonade most of the day, while Jim patiently lugged planks and bricks to fashion makeshift stands.

There were other happenings too that demonstrated Judy's connection with the written word. There was the April that she persuaded me to lend the use of my big galvanized tub for the tadpoles she brought home from the creek.

"It'll be a good Science project, mom! I read about it at school. Maybe Diane can put hers in it too…"

Diane and Phil and several others added to the collection until there must have been two hundred wriggling tadpoles in the tub. And then of course, they were suddenly transposed. Those tiny frogs hopped out of their watery home, infiltrating the yard like giant land logged mosquitoes while I walked gingerly about, flinching at occasional crunching sounds underfoot. The Science project was over.

The episode, though, that really involved our whole family in a way that we never forgot was the Easter chick giveaway. It began innocently enough with a small ad in the

Chicken Hearted

Los Gatos Times.

FREE CHICKS, THE PERFECT EASTER GIFT. HALF A DOZEN CUDDLY CHICKS FOR YOUR CHILD.

"Can I get some Mom? Please. They're so cute."

"Who'd take care of them? They get bigger, you know."

"Oh, I would—I'd feed them and give them water. I promise."

"Well, I'll talk to Daddy."

In the back of my mind was a vision of fresh brown eggs, perhaps a stewing hen later to simmer on a cold winter's day. Carefully, I approached Jim with the idea.

"That'll be the day when she gets up early enough to feed chickens!. She's always running out the door at the last minute as it is." I knew Jim had raised chickens as a child. He had told me about gathering eggs for breakfast.

"Might be good training for her though. I guess I could rig up a pen with some of the left-over chicken wire."

Persuading Jim had proved easier than I thought. When I told Judy, she was ecstatic.

"Oh, Mommy! I'm going to tell Debby—maybe her mother will let her have some too!"

Fine, I thought. As long as it's in their backyard.

Not only did Debby get six chicks, so did her little sister, Pamela. And if Pamela did, Jimmy must have six also. Judy would care for his. Oh well, what's a dozen I thought. They're little.

For a week, eighteen month old Jimmy sat entranced outside the chicken wire pen circled on the ground, while Judy played with or fed the ever-hungry chicks. His eyes darted as fast as the rapidly moving bodies as they jostled each other for food and water. I congratulated myself for giving Judy the new responsibility. She was getting up earlier and hadn't missed the bus once.

On the day after Easter, Judy said to me:

"Mommy, Debby and Pammy want to give us their chickens. Their mother says she can't take care of them and the new baby too, and they don't want them anymore. If we don't take them, they'll die!"

I bowed to the inevitable.

Six weeks and twenty-four chickens later, the sound of crowing woke me every morning at sunup. They all crowed. My vision of brown eggs and gentle clucking hens had vanished. The fluffy little chicks had vanished too, metamorphosed into scrawny, molting, hungry roosters. Judy still fed and watered them faithfully, running back and forth from the garage where the feed was kept to the pen Jim had built in the backyard. I could hear her quick steps through the open kitchen window as I prepared breakfast. Sometimes I could hear her high-pitched voice as she scattered food for them, calling each by name. "Here Tommy. That's a good boy, Twinky."

And later, "Mom, we have to buy more food. They eat so much..."

"Honey, the neighbors are beginning to complain about the roosters' crowing so early in the morning. It's getting louder every day. We have to find a solution."

A day or so later, Jim gave Judy the ultimatum. "We'll have to kill them when they're twelve weeks old. They'll be the right size then to put in the freezer."

Surprisingly, there was no outcry. Six more weeks seemed far away to Judy and she went about her schedule as usual. Doomsdays are easy to ignore.

Finally, on a sunny June Saturday, the family was in place for the chicken slaughter. Neither Jim nor I expected Judy to take any part in it and she had shut herself in her bedroom with the shades drawn. Jim was to be the executioner, I the feather plucker and eviscerator. Even before it all began, I wished the day were over.

Jim had never killed a chicken. We did not own an axe.

"How are you going to kill them without an axe? I remember Dad always used one." I asked, remembering too how the chickens ran around the yard in circles after their heads were cut off. I shuddered.

"Well, I've got it figured out. I'll put some feed on the grass in this circle where I've got it marked with twine." I'd wondered about the loop of brown twine with the brick in the center. "Then I'll bring out one chicken at a time and lure it into the circle with the feed. I'll grab it and put its head on the brick and cut it off, nice and neat. It won't feel anything. Is the knife good and sharp?"

I watched from the sanctuary of the kitchen where I waited beside the pot of boiling water that was to be the next step in the process. I saw Jim lure a rooster into the magic circle, grab it and throw it down near the brick, kitchen knife in hand: saw him bring the knife to the feathered neck, then step back quickly, again two sure steps toward the bird, again the quick retreat. It's like dancing the cha cha, I thought, one-two-cha-cha-cha. Jim turned suddenly and walked toward the kitchen.

"I can't do it. I've gotta have a drink. Maybe if I have a drink..."

I watched him slug down a shot of bourbon. Back in the yard, the process was repeated. This time he managed to cut the neck. I could see the blood, but the head remained intact. Jim came in for another drink. I decided to stop watching. A few moments later, a warm feathered carcass was laid in the kitchen sink. It was time for me to go to work.

After that, I didn't watch much. Chickens kept appearing and I heard the cupboard door where the bourbon was kept, as it slammed shut several more times. Somewhere in the bedroom region, Judy was sobbing and crying out,

"Murderer! Murderer!" Jimmy was crying too, awakened from his nap.

Jim came into the kitchen. "Mel came over. He saw me over the fence. He's killed a lot of chickens. He showed me how to wring their necks. It's easier—no blood. I'm getting the hang of it. Fourteen more to go!"

I stood ankle deep in feathers, grateful to our next-door neighbor. I felt back in some nightmare cannery scene, dipping the birds in boiling water, pulling feathers, cutting off heads and feet and eviscerating the surprisingly small bodies. It would take two of them to make a meal. Judy was sitting in her darkened bedroom, whispering to Jimmy, holding him and crying no longer. At least they're quiet, I thought. Poor Judy. Poor Jim, having to kill them. Poor me with all this mess. Poor chicks... My body moved in rhythm: counter, kettle, floor, sink. Jim had finished his job and was gathering up the newspapers full of feathers and entrails for the garbage.

"Mama Mia—what a day!" He stumbled a little as he carried out the trash.

Finally, the job was done. Judy and Jimmy had ventured into the dining room to stare through the kitchen door for the last twenty minutes, while I finished bagging the chickens. Their eyes were wide at the sight of feathers and chicken bodies.

"Would you like to see the inside of a chicken? Here's the heart, and the gizzard—see the sand? That's where all the food is digested. And here's the liver—you can tell your teacher how much you've learned today."

There was no response from Judy. It would be a long time before she assimilated today's lessons. A long time for me too.

THE HARVEST

I stood in the middle of the kitchen on a hot August day, surveying the piles of over-ripe peaches in the sink and wiping the perspiration from my forehead with the corner of my apron. Little Jimmy was happily making a tower of blocks on the kitchen table, while eighteen month old Cathy busily toddled around the living room, pulling every book and magazine onto the floor from their accustomed shelves. The smell of bubbling peach juice emanated from the oven and I peeked to see if the crusts on the four pies inside were brown enough to take them out to cool.

Four more pies were ready to slip onto the oven racks as soon as they were cleared of their present load. I could then assemble another four while the fresh batch baked.

It was summer harvest time, and I was a slave to *THE HARVEST*, a vegetable stand Jim and his erstwhile partner, Al Walker, had built across from *Rickey's* restaurant on El Camino Real in Palo Alto.

Owning our own business had all seemed so perfect at first. Jim was at his most animated when he talked to me about his dream of ownership but opportunities were rare at the San Jose Ice Co. where he was a salesman. The advent of Al Walker, a retired businessman from Seattle, and his wife Polly, into our lives had presented the opportunity Jim was waiting for. We'd all met at the Presbyterian Church in San Jose and had become friends. Al had money to invest: Jim had youthful energy and intelligence to give. It was a classic and seemingly perfect situation.

"I've got $20,000 I can put into something that can make us some money," Al told Jim one day.

"I've got an idea," Jim said. "Just let me think about it a little more." And he did have an idea. His contact with the grocery stores he dealt with in the ice business had taught him how much housewives prized fresh fruits and vegetables. It was a trend inspired by newly health conscious young *Sunset* magazine readers, home during the day with their new homes and growing families.

"It's a natural," Jim told me one evening. "We could open a fruit stand; buy vegetables and fruit from the farmers around here. Al will put up the money for a building and we've found a good location. He can help me run the place."

"You'd have to quit your job," I said with a sense of foreboding. I remembered times during the Depression when there was no income for our family and that unease was still a part of me. "Isn't that a little risky?"

"I could keep working while they're building the store. But yes, I would quit once *The Harvest* gets going. How do you like that name? Al thought it up, and I think it really fits."

I did too. It seemed symbolic of all the things we'd worked for in the last few years, a chance to capitalize on the anxiety of the War years and the hard work of building our house. I had never seen Jim so excited over a project.

The building was a long, low concrete block structure with a large work and storage room in the back and an extended, protecting roof in front underneath which the fruits and vegetables would be displayed. A large sign, THE HARVEST showed prominently on the roof. On the first of May 1952, the display cases fully stocked, Jim and Al were open for business.

All had gone well at first. During the busy summer months, when supplies were plentiful, the two men worked well together. Jim had made contacts with several suppliers—Shig, a Japanese American farmer out on Brokaw Rd could always be counted on for the biggest most flavorful strawberries; apricots and cherries were available locally. The almost new Dodge pickup truck Jim bought was perfect for trips to the Valley for peaches in August. While the profits were not quite as great as the men envisioned, they were content. "It'll build up the longer we stay there," Jim assured me.

Winter had proved a different story. The colorful displays of fruits and fresh vegetables gave way to lettuces, cabbages, squashes, potatoes, certainly desirable, but not as eye-catching as the summer's storefront had been. The concrete block building was chilly and Al came down with a bad cold, which hung on for weeks. "I'll be home late," Jim said often that winter. "Al's not feeling so good."

As spring came on, still chilly and windy, Al took to walking around and around the building, shaking his head with worry. "I dunno. We're not taking in much money," he'd say dolefully to Jim.

"I don't know what's bugging him," Jim told me. "He

doesn't need the money and he knows it takes time..."

By late spring, Al was wanting out. "This isn't what I had in mind," he said one day. "You'll have to buy me out."

Jim was aghast. Our finances certainly did not support the idea of buying a business. That hadn't been the bargain. But Al was as persistent as water dripping on stone, complaining and sighing over his so-called predicament.

One day, he'd said to Jim, "You can buy me out for six thousand. I've got it figured out that what with the partnership and all the work you've put in here, that would be a fair price."

Looking back now, I think what a piddling amount of money that was, but in 1953 six thousand dollars was worth at least sixty thousand in today's currency. Not a piddling amount for a young family to take on. The entire process visibly upset Jim who was losing weight and sleeping poorly at night. Borrowing money was not in his scheme of things.

Eventually, though, we had decided it was the only answer and the necessary loan was made. We were now sole owners of *The Harvest* and I was doing all I could to help, which in this case meant baking pies. Jim took them with him in the mornings, sometimes taking twelve year old Judy along as well to help in any way she could. My recollection is that we sold the pies for seventy-five cents apiece, though that seems an incredibly low amount, but again factoring in today's prices, it may have been normal. In any case, they sold readily and I baked to keep up with the almost-too-ripe fruit Jim brought home in the evenings.

Jim's brother, Tom, had come out from Pennsylvania to help him in the store, since Al was no longer available. Tom was Jim's eldest brother, a slender, muscular man with a ready smile. Where I had resented brother Bob's visit, I enjoyed Tom. He was a handsome man, looking much like Jim with his brown eyes and firm jaw. His slightly graying hair gave softness to his features, which Jim lacked. Always ready to compliment me on my cooking, kind and gentle with the children, I enjoyed having him at our table. Jim had become so used to my cooking that he seldom commented on it and I basked in the appreciation Tom voiced. The two men often got up at three a.m. to drive to Lodi or Stockton to get a load of peaches before the day's business during this fecund time of the year.

Jim was finding, though, that his anticipated profit from the business was not as much as he'd planned for. The markup could only be a small amount in order to keep prices level with the competition. "If we only had our own ranch like the Cosentino family does," he said. "There's no middleman to deal with and they can sell cheap and still make more profit."

We were noticing too, that the housewives who cared so much about fresh fruits and vegetables were apt to buy them at the supermarkets, which had become more and more plentiful, along with the milk and eggs and cereal and other items they needed. Jim did get fresh eggs from a local farmer, but basic groceries were beyond his power to stock and sell. And lettuce did spoil, along with tomatoes and the other summer perishables that remained unsold. Having your own business wasn't all it was cracked up to be!

We hung on that winter, one of the worst in recent memory, while Judy cracked walnuts in the evening after her homework was done, putting the meats into plastic bags to sell. Tom returned to Blairsville. Jim manned the store by himself, driving home on the cold winter nights after nightfall. I thought of making homemade mincemeat or fruitcake for the holiday season, but somehow that project never came to fruition.

The next summer, brother John arrived from Blairsville, another stalwart and pleasant helper for Jim during the busy summer months. Again I made pies, starting earlier in the season with apricots. I saw little of my neighbors that season, busy as I was with baking, childcare, gardening—Jim didn't have time for anything but the business—and worrying about finances. He had been forced to borrow money from his father in order to keep afloat with his suppliers, and I wondered what the winter would bring. Don't borrow trouble, I said to myself as I peeled apples in September for more pies.

By early November, Jim was ready to throw in the towel, put *The Harvest* on the market or just close the doors and walk away from it. "I hate to be a quitter," he said one day, "but I can't keep throwing good money after bad. I'll find something else to do…"

Again the clutch of uncertainty tightened my chest with anxiety. If only I could work, I thought, but how, with two little kids? I looked at the mountains visible from our windows and tried to remember that there were larger vistas of life than the one I saw right now. This too will pass, I told myself, thinking of Mother's often-repeated words during the Depression years.

Mother and Dad usually drove out to our house on

Sunday after church. They didn't stay long as a rule and while Mother and I chatted, Dad loved to just sit and watch the children play, or talk with Jim about the latest 49er game. One Sunday, just before Thanksgiving, Dad was in a jovial mood,

"Hey, Jim," he said. "I heard IBM is putting up a new plant here in Campbell, over on Dell Ave. And they're hiring." Dad had recently retired from IBM, where he'd always been enthusiastic about the company. "I told them what a good worker you are. Why don't you go over and apply?"

And that is exactly what Jim did. Little did we know then that Jim's new job would make him a loyal IBM-er for the next thirty years; that he would rise from a swing shift card punch operator to an instructor, enthusiastically teaching new employees all over the country. All we knew was that *The Harvest* building was turned into a real estate office, and that the trials of that period would become a part of our family history. Only in time would we realize our real harvest was in the security of a steady income and the means to provide for a growing family.

THE FIRST BIRD

Teenagers began to come into their own in the mid 1950's, and I was caught utterly unprepared for the vast change in manners and habits that had occurred since I was in that category. Judy was fifteen, a sophomore in high school, with a host of girl friends. They seemed to know exactly when her foot entered the door of our home, evidenced by the immediate ringing of the telephone, a ringing that went on all evening.

My admonitions that homework should not be interrupted were rudely rebuffed. Any suggestion I made regarding suitable clothing for different occasions was ignored. Judy, whose Principal in grade school had told us she was the brightest student in the school, now barely got by in her studies.

Looking back, I can view the changes that took place with a degree of equanimity, knowing that such "rebellion" was normal, but in those days there were no groups of parents to commiserate with over the antics of teenagers. There were no magazine articles. No books for parents to refer to. Dr. Spock didn't go that far. My daughter was at least five years older than the children in our neighborhood;

their parents had yet to encounter the first rebellious act for which they must set standards. I had no one to talk to.

Also, in those days, one did not talk about family problems with others. One was supposed to solve problems within the family. The day of counselors and therapists had not arrived. And we did have a problem in our family. From the time our son Jimmy was born, Jim's attitude toward Judy had changed. He was no longer the loving Daddy to the adorable little girl he had so willingly adopted, but a cold, undemonstrative father to a skinny eight and half year old, who needed his reassuring love even more. The following years had not improved the situation, and by the time Judy reached fifteen, her anger touched not only her father but me as well.

Actually, Judy's rebellion was almost entirely verbal. Drugs had not come onto the scene in the mid 1950's; alcohol was not in the picture. Her belittling remarks to her friends about my hairdo, my clothing, my shoes, rankled. I particularly remember snide remarks about some green shoes I wore, which probably were as ugly as her sneering indicated. Had I not been so preoccupied with three younger children, whom she adored, and with being a buffer between her and Jim, I probably would have laughed. But my only frame of reference was my own youth and relationship with my mother, whom I had never reviled in any way.

Mealtimes became so tense I could barely wait to get through them, with Judy talking about some happening or other at school and Jim eating silently, a frown on his face. I remember one incident when Judy stayed too long on the phone with a friend and Jim yelled at her that he would "pull the phone off the wall" if she didn't hang up, whereupon she shouted,

"I hate you—I hate you!" and Jim slapped her face, hard.

After that traumatic experience, I did persuade Jim to go with me to our pediatrician who was doing a little family counseling, but when I complained about Jim's gruff voice when talking to Judy, the doctor merely replied,

"Well, if that's Jim's usual way of talking to her, Judy should be used to it by now," thereby reinforcing Jim's conviction that he was right and that Judy and I were complaining unnecessarily. We never went back.

Those were hard times, and I often thought about the irony of the choice I had made in deciding to marry Jim when it seemed so important to me to have a father for Judy. Life had screwed me up, and if it had not been for the joy of the younger children, and my stubborn insistence that the unity of the family was more important than any one individual, I would not have known how to cope. As it was, I managed to see to it that Judy's friendships, so important to her, remained intact, mostly by being a buffer between her and Jim. Though I never spoke of my inner turmoil to my friends, just being with them helped to take my mind off the tension at home.

When Judy, our first bird out of the nest, went away to Pasadena Junior college life at home eased. Jimmy was nine years old, Cathy seven and Joan three. Jim was doing well at IBM and I kept busy as a Brownie leader, Sunday School teacher and President of the Parent Teacher's Association.

Judy blossomed that year too, finding college an outlet for her intellectual and social needs. When the entire family drove to Pasadena to bring her home in early June, we were in for a treat.

I had gotten in touch with my friend from high school days, Donnabelle Mullenger who was now the famous movie star, Donna Reed. Donna invited our family to watch the filming of an episode of "The Donna Reed Show", one our family watched regularly. Ida Lupino was directing that day; Carl Betz, Paul Petersen and Shelley Fabares as well as Donna were "on." The entire cast and crew were solicitous of our comfort, insisting we sit near the front in comfortable chairs and the young stars, Paul and Shelley each came over to chat with my children. It was thrilling moment for each of them.

I will never forget the sight of Donna walking on the sidewalk in front of Jim and me, hand in hand with our two youngest daughters, while Jimmy and Judy followed closely behind. At lunch, devouring hamburgers in a "joint" not far from the studio, Donna and I caught up on the details of old friends and our families. It all seemed so natural—that's the kind of person Donna was. That's the way we Iowans are.

That first year of college had mellowed both Judy and Jim, and though they never became really easy in each other's company, life at home was smoother. Jim helped Judy get a job for the summer as a card punch operator in the same IBM plant where he worked, a position she was to keep in the summers that followed and which helped with her school expenses.

I remember one evening that first summer when Judy said to me—

"Daddy makes me so mad! You should see him at work, Mom! He's always joking with people and they really like him. He's never like that here at home. I feel like we're cheated."

It was true. Jim *was* a different person out in the world. I'd noticed the same thing at social events. I had spoken to him about it, but there didn't seem to be anything he could do about his dour attitude at home. I'd learned to accept it.

But Judy was flying on her own now, and the two of us were again the mother and daughter friends and confidants I had been afraid were lost forever.

COMFORT FOOD

There was a rainy, chilly Saturday in November of 1970 when I badly needed comfort. My daughter, Cathryn, was nineteen, a freshman at San Jose State University. The Vietnam War was still in progress, and Cathy was in love with a young man we'd barely met, Art Gonzales. Art was in the Army, soon to be shipped out and they were determined to marry before he left.

I was, of course, appalled. She was so *young*, only nineteen! No matter that I'd been a mother at the same age. In fact, remembering those troubled years of my own youth, I was determined that she not rush into an early marriage. I wanted her to have time to experience life more fully before making such a serious decision. I'd lain awake in the early hours of morning for many nights worrying about what such a momentous and sudden decision might do to my daughter's future. But Cathryn had a will of her own, and had said to me, "Mom, if we can't have a wedding, we'll just get married anyway. We can always drive to Reno, you know."

I did know. I'd exhausted my ammunition.

"O.K. Set a date," I said. "You can talk to Reverend

Boswell and make the church arrangements." We would
have the wedding at our church, the Los Gatos Methodist,
and our minister would officiate.

So it was that on this November day I was making
a wedding dress, with as good spirits as I could muster.
The wedding would be in three weeks and Cathy would
be a beautiful bride. A dear friend had lent us her daughter's exquisite lace mantilla, brought back from Spain for
her own wedding the past June. I would make a simple,
form fitting white satin dress to set off the mantilla. To
honor Art's Mexican-American family a colorful affair was
planned. The bridesmaids would wear bright flower pat-
terned long skirts and silk blouses in a deep rose color.

I'd brought the sewing machine into the living room
where the south facing windows would catch any sunshine that might come during the rainy day. Jim built a fire
in the fireplace: I started minestrone soup in the kettle on
the stove.

The stage was set for rising spirits, but they had yet to
arrive in me. Tension tightened my chest, and I took a deep
breath as I laid out the lovely satin carefully; made the first
cuts in the fabric. Soon I was stitching the first seam, then
another and another.

To my surprise, I found myself singing, "I'm Always
Chasing Rainbows" over and over under my breath. My
shoulders eased as some of the tension left after Cathy's
first "try on". The dress fit perfectly. I decided to take
a break and make an apple pie. I loved making pies on
Saturdays. It was a link to my mother who always baked
on Saturdays for Sunday's dinner.

By the end of the afternoon, the dress was finished with

only the hand sewing left to do—the hem, the tiny pearl buttons on the long sleeves. Cathy was delighted with the result. "Mom, its so beautiful—thank you, thank you!"

Whenever I think of that day, the sound of the crackling fire, the hum of the sewing machine, the blended odors of the vegetables in the minestrone, and the cinnamon in the apple pie come back to me. It was a day for hope and love and the good smells and sounds of home, after all.

The wedding was perfect, Art handsome in a tuxedo and Cathy a radiant bride. Cathy's sister Judy was matron of honor, sister Joan and one of Art's sisters-in-law, bridesmaids. Ron Gerard sang "Ode to Joy" and Bob Boswell beamed as he introduced "Mr. And Mrs. Arthur Gonzales" to the assembled guests.

I wish I could report that my premonitions were faulty; that the marriage lasted for these thirty years. As I had feared, such was not the case. Cathy and Art divorced after the Vietnam War ended and he had come back home. We have lost touch with Art over the years. Cathy did marry again and she and her beloved Mike just celebrated their fifteenth year of happy marriage.

The term "comfort food" has come into its own recently. My guess is that the American diet has become so diversified, so accustomed to a wide variety of choices of ethnic foods, that anything that reminds us of our childhood favorites has become "comfort". For a Chinese/American that might be pot stickers or winter melon soup; for a Latino, tamales. You get the idea.

My comfort foods tend toward vegetable soups, hearty

beef stews, baking powder biscuits with butter and honey, apple pie or a coconut cake. It takes a certain kind of day to bring out the comfort food yen in me—cloudy skies, pouring rain, a chill in the air. Some emotional climates produce the same effect.

If I am feeling restless, or sad; puzzled over a problem or simply out of sorts, a cooking project gives me focus. If I am browning meat for a stew to be simmered for hours with the good smell of carrots and onions wafting through the house, my blocked energy has found an outlet.

Today is a case in point. An April shower made me decide against walking the two miles I like to traverse on mornings when I don't swim. I decided to bake bread instead to go with the pot of lima bean soup I'd already planned to make for dinner. In former years I would have made the bread from scratch, kneading it vigorously, letting it rise, kneading and rising again before shaping it into loaves to bake golden in the oven. Now, I use a bread machine to do the kneading and rising for me. I have never become accustomed to cylindrical loaves of bread with the paddle incision from the machine baked into it, so I always set the control for "Dough" and remove the dough when the machine tells me to. Then I place the dough in a regular bread pan to rise again and finally bake in the oven. True, I have to pay more attention with this method but I'm convinced of its worth.

If you'd like to try the lima bean soup, this is the way I made it today. It is simply soaked limas, covered with cold water and simmered with a beef bouillon cube for forty minutes; then a chopped onion, three carrots and two ribs of celery also chopped, added along with a half pound of cubed ham. It will simmer another forty minutes and the flavors will be deliciously blended by dinnertime.

I guess the little girl who salivated over Tarzan's raw lion meat, or Heidi's bread and cheese when she read about them while sitting in the swing on a summer afternoon, still lurks somewhere within me. Just writing about food makes me comfortable!

*Judy and "Daddy Jim"
in Lumberton, S.C.
1943.*

*Our little tap dancer,
Judy 1944.*

*Jim in "civvies" – home
at last. 1945.*

With brothers Paul (in uniform) and Bob in 1944.

Jim and his "girls". Left to right, Me, Joan, Judy and Cathy about 1969.

Donna Reed & I at "Mothers for Peace" meeting in San Francisco.

Four generations, 1970. Clockwise, Juliana, Katherine, Lindsey, Judy

NEW LIFE YEARS

Stepping Out

There were many reasons that I left Jim Cardellino after thirty-two years of marriage and four grown children. I can give all of them, but to be perfectly honest, the final push was the love affair I was having with being able to dance again. The passion to move to music that I had discovered a way to indulge colored my definition of myself. It affected every plan I made.

It had come about when Fred Gordon, a long time and trusted friend, caught up with me at a neighborhood wedding, an outdoor affair bright with sunshine, good spirits and plenty of wine. I may have been wearing a red wig that day—wigs were big in 1974, especially among bored housewives whose families were leaving the nest and whose jobs had grown stale along with their marriages. It was true that an occasion like this brought out the best, the optimistic, and the self-congratulatory glow in many of the couples present. We'd all survived many years together, but underneath it all, at least in my case, there was a sense that life had short changed me.

I had been thinking a lot about death the last few years. Not, heaven forbid, with any sense of causing my own but in a more philosophic way. My father's death in 1960 at the age of seventy two and my mother's subsequent lonely widowhood were reminders of life's brevity. How was I going to grow old with Jim with his increased drinking, his angry moods, our inability to converse, and his self-absorption? His antagonism toward Judy and her husband, even though I tried to hide it from them, was always present. Even the new little granddaughter, Lindsey, got no more than a grudging nod from Jim. It was an undercurrent in my life that flowed like a muddy stream under the clear sparkling persona I presented to the world.

So when Freddy, in an expansive moment, said to me that bright day

"Juliana, the next time Jim goes out of town on a trip for IBM, would you like to go dancing with me?" My eager smile gave him the answer.

Fred and I had often danced at neighborhood parties when our families were present. It had always been the highlight of the evening for me. Doubt must have shown in my face when I thought of Jim's reaction to such a plan, for Freddy quickly added—

"I'll go over right now and ask Jim if he'd mind—"

Which is exactly what he did. I could see the two men conversing; see Jim's nod and smile and knew that somehow this was really going to happen. I was going to go dancing again!

It came about three weeks later when Jim was away on a teaching trip for IBM. Several years earlier he had begun this new career within the giant company that he loved, when his immediate superior had mentioned the possibility of undertaking a teaching position.

"I think you'd be a natural, Jim. What they want is someone to teach classes for new employees in different parts of the country. Explain how the company works, what our attitudes are, and some specifics for certain positions. You're always so enthusiastic about the company—think about it."

It was true. Jim did love his job at Big Blue. In the twenty years since he had started working swing shift at the Card plant in Campbell as a cardpunch operator, he had advanced in the company. His position in the office had brought more responsibilities and he often worked overtime. I remembered the day he had sought my advice about changing from his machine-operating duties at the Card plant to a less lucrative one in the office.

"I won't make as much—I'll be working days instead of nights. I don't know if working in the office is worth making less money."

"I think you should do it, honey," I'd said. "You'll be with a different class of people, with more chance for advancement. We can get by on less for awhile." And we had. The salary I earned as a medical assistant to a local surgeon would help, especially with the "extras" the girls, Cathy and Joan, needed for their dance and piano lessons.

Jim, to my surprise, was an excellent teacher and I found, even more to my surprise, that I loved the times when he was away; those weeks when I was really my own boss with only the children and myself to think about. The homecomings were pleasant too, when Jim could boast about the raves he'd gotten from his students and co-workers, even though I felt cheated when his interest in my activities during his absence got short shrift. I liked the rush of affection I felt when he returned: the warmth of sex after his absence.

I was exhilarated by the fun of my first dance "date" with Freddy and as the summer wore on, I continued to meet him at the dance hall on Friday evenings. Our "dates" were strictly platonic, with Freddy escorting me up the stairs to the second floor ballroom in San Jose, dancing a few numbers together, and then taking me safely back to my car again at the end of the evening. I said little about those evenings to Jim and he never questioned me about them.

Once or twice, when Jim was home on a Friday night, he'd consent to go to the ballroom himself. But his grudging acceptance of the music and the dancing took the edge off the fun. And I had to dance every dance with him, which was great for the waltz but boring for the swing and the cha cha. I loved dancing a fast swing number with Freddy, doing a lively sugar-push or fast twirls to the beat. I loved the challenge of new partners, trying to match my steps to theirs, having them compliment me on my following ability. I felt young and pretty and desirable in the soft lights, even though I was a fifty-something year old.

Our children were pretty much grown and on their own. Joan, our youngest was at the University, living in Berkeley. Son Jim had graduated from San Jose State University and was working as a counselor in a home for emotionally disturbed teenagers. Daughter Cathy was working too. Judy, recently retired from her teaching job, was a new mother to our first grandchild. I'd been a responsible mother since I was eighteen and it was time for me to kick up my heels—literally.

I was still employed, but taking time to attend some classes at our local Junior College. This was an opportunity to indulge in subjects I'd never before had time for: ceramics, philosophy, and music appreciation. I had a plan in mind to cut my working hours down next year to take more classes: I loved the exchange of ideas with teachers and students. I'd even met an old friend from the San Jose Presbyterian Church days who'd started classes too.

Our marriage was changing. I was stepping out into the world, finding new freedoms, and Jim was becoming more reclusive.

Part of that change had occurred a year or so before. Jim was still teaching and we had joined an organization called "Creative Initiative Foundation", (CIF) a group dedicated to making marriages—and hence service to the community—stronger. A friend had talked Jim into attending the first meeting, and he'd taken to it and its confrontational style with ease. As for me, I grew to love the fact that someone else could ask the hard questions about our relationship that had bothered me for years. Questions like why we almost never laughed together; or why, in general, we really didn't enjoy the same things. Why just being quietly with one another didn't produce inner tranquility: why I felt so lonely in my marriage.

The annual CIF spring retreat in Ben Lomond was one both of us responded to and planned to attend, but the small print restrictions had escaped Jim's notice. Liquor was forbidden and when I brought up the issue after having put off mentioning it to him, Jim balked. Jim "needed" his "relaxing" drinks.

"Nobody's gonna tell me whether I can drink or not!" he said angrily. "What business is it of theirs?"

When I protested that it was part of the group's philosophy not to indulge in artificial stimuli, he just grunted. I was afraid he'd back out at the last moment, as he'd done so many times in the past when he had agreed to a social event and cancelled in a sudden pique at the last moment, leaving me to explain his absence by pleading a sudden case of "flu".

My hopes for the weekend, which I had fantasized would bring us closer together, were dashed. We had been able to talk more intimately than ever before since we'd been in CIF, but I was afraid it was a temporary situation. I was used to Jim changing his mind about social commitments we'd made, but this was different.

But Jim had a vested interest too. He'd grown to like some of the men at the biweekly meetings. They respected his ability to ask tough questions when a man or woman was reluctant to share hidden emotions. And he was enthusiastic about the group's goals.

"O.K.—I'll go. But I've got to leave before it's over. I've got to catch a plane real early Monday morning." He muttered something about vodka under his breath and left the room. Taking a deep breath, I packed.

The weekend did go well. By the time Jim was preparing to leave the group on Sunday I felt we had come very close to the heart of my questions. We were talking more freely, more honestly with each other, than ever before.

"I wish you didn't have to go…"

"But I have to. I told you before…" He hurriedly stuffed

shirts into his bag, gave me a quick kiss and was out the door.

Jim's departure felt like an escape, a running from me and the organization and my yearnings for a closer relationship. I felt abandoned.

"It must feel lonely to be here by yourself," one woman said to me and with that the floodgates of emotion, which I had tried so hard to control, broke and I began to cry. I'll never forget those wracking uncontrollable sobs. I could not go back to the bleakness of the way we'd been!

A few weeks later, Jim announced that he no longer wanted to be part of CIF. "You can go if you want, but I don't want to put the time and effort into it any more."

I knew that Jim would not change his mind and that my going to meetings alone was impossible. The organization only accepted couples. I decided to continue looking for answers to my questions on my own.

I searched out a counselor in Menlo Park and went to see her on a weekly basis. I read self-help book after self-help book: *Games People Play; I'm O.K. You're O.K.*, many more. I couldn't get enough of them. I'll be so glad when I can get interested in a regular book again, I thought one day as I drove for a meeting with my counselor. I'm tired of thinking about me and my problems! But I kept going, and found my inner tension lessening as I strove to talk honestly about my life. One day the counselor said, almost idly, "There's always the option of divorce, you know."

I felt as though a door had opened with sunshine streaming in. Here was permission to have thoughts I'd pushed away for years. I wasn't yet ready for such radical action, but I did begin to consider the possibility of living alone for a time. Maybe separation would clarify our situation.

One beautiful sun-shot day, when driving home from a session, I had a breakthrough. *I alone was responsible for my life! I didn't have to make decisions to please others—I should make them to please myself! And be responsible for them!* Why I had never before realized that rather obvious truth puzzled me, but I had learned enough to know I'd been raised to be a "good girl" and to put others' wishes ahead of my own; to care deeply about outsiders' opinions of me. I resolved to change my behavior from *I should* to *I want.* It all sounds very 70's but the insight was a milestone for me.

It's painful to dredge up these old memories. I don't want to think again of those scenes of sullen silences, of me crouching in a fetal position between our twin beds unable to deal with another of Jim's angry outbursts, and wishing I could yell and scream back at him like our neighbor across the street did when her husband came home drunk. I don't like the twinges of guilt I still sometimes feel when I think maybe I could have done more—been more understanding, more accepting. Jim had been a good provider and loyal husband and father for thirty-two years. Why couldn't I just keep on as I'd been doing?

But I couldn't face growing old with so much anger, so little warmth between us to nourish me. I wanted to study more without incurring rancor; wanted to keep our old friends that Jim now forbade me to have in our home when he was present. I wanted to live my life listening to the music of it, not the black undertones. I wanted to dance to my life!

In August of 1975 I moved into an apartment of my

own, determined to find out if life was better that way. If it weren't, if I found I'd been a fool and couldn't get along without Jim, I would swallow my pride and return to my marriage and my home.

I never did go back, but I did dance. I danced with Fred and with strangers at the YMCA Singles dances, strangers who sometimes became friends, occasionally lovers. My life was like a dance then, full of twists and turns: the dark undertones of a slinking Tango or the abandoned joy of a Swing.

I followed the drumbeat of necessity, getting a teaching credential and finding a position teaching medical assistants in a vocational school. Later, when teaching hours did not bring in enough income, I took a job as a medical assistant myself, at a large hospital in Santa Clara.

I followed the subtle music of sun and wind, the laughter and talk of friends, as I spent Sundays hiking the foothills and mountains of the San Francisco Bay area of California with a Sierra Club group. And, finally, after six years of living alone, I danced surely and joyfully into a new life with Emil Richmond, matching my steps with his in every way.

RICH

On Halloween of 1979, a Thursday, I drove north from my home in Santa Clara to Palo Alto for an evening of dancing. I had, as usual, spent the day working in the OB-GYN section of the local Kaiser Clinic, mostly ushering pregnant young women into examining rooms, weighing them, taking their blood pressure, making them feel comfortable. Some I'd gotten to know during the months of their pregnancies, some were new and nervous; frequently I needed to search out an interpreter for a woman who spoke only Spanish.

Fortunately, there had been no abortion clinic that day. I hated ushering the young teenagers into their exam rooms for the initial visit. The abortion part didn't bother me—I was glad they had the opportunity to get their lives back on track. What did make me sad were the ones who, when asked if they planned to use birth control in the future, said "Oh no! That would ruin the romance!" I knew they would be back.

Working at Kaiser was interesting, demanding, sometimes boring. Most of my co-workers were far younger than I and often their chatter about boyfriends, young children and husbands left me feeling isolated. While they gathered in one of the exam rooms to lunch and gossip every day, I usually took a walk or retreated to an empty office to read. I was fifty-eight years old, supporting myself with the only training I had, that of being a medical assistant. True, I had a teaching degree, but it was for vocational teaching only, and I couldn't support myself on the hours available for that job.

So I put in the workdays as pleasantly as possible, thankful for the bright note of my immediate boss, a beautiful young Pakistani doctor who had recently joined the staff. I could talk with her, and with some of the nurses in the Clinic about other things: travel, books, and life experiences.

All that was my daytime life. Tuesdays, Thursdays and Saturdays were my Cinderella nights. My dragging energies when I walked into my apartment door after a day's work were magically transformed as I bathed and dressed for the evening out, not to attend a ball, but to go to a "singles" dance at one of the YMCA's in Palo Alto. We seniors were luckier than many young folks, I thought, for we had a place to dance and meet others in a friendly and safe environment. Living alone as I did, dancing provided more than moving to music: I could be held close to a partner; feel his body, hold his hand. I could smile with inner joy and forget long workdays and empty nights, all without commitment for more than the moment. .

Tonight was to be a Halloween party, and I had hastily dressed in a long black skirt and bright blouse. I was wearing every necklace in my jewel box, a colorful assortment of "junk" jewelry. My arms clinked with bracelets; I had put on the biggest pair of hoop earrings I owned, completing the costume of a gypsy woman. Not very original, I thought, but it would do.

I felt happy as I drove. The setting October sun was lower in the sky at this hour of seven than it had been in the summer when its fierce blaze of farewell to the day shone so brightly in my eyes I could barely see to drive. Last summer had been tough; a time of moods when I drove to the dances thinking how many years will I spend driving the freeway like this? The thought had filled me with a dread I did not dare look at too closely. .

I'd been living alone for five years, and still when one of my children or a friend shut the door of my apartment at the end of a visit, a momentary pang of loneliness hit me like a stone in my chest. Of course I compensated with work, these dances, friends, hiking with a Sierra Club singles group, dates. But always underneath was the quest for someone to share my life. Someone to talk with, laugh with, and dance with: someone to care about. It would happen someday, I told myself.

There had been one man who fulfilled many of my requirements. He not only danced, he took me to the symphony: an engineer who studied Law in night school. Maybe he's the one, I'd thought, but he'd already been married five times and I sensed hidden flaws. After six months of knowing each other, it turned out I didn't fit his requirements—I wasn't Jewish! So I was back to driving the freeway alone several nights a week.

On this night, though, just wearing a costume put me in a festive mood. and when I entered the dance hall, I stepped happily with my first partner into the roomful of swirling couples. Swing, waltz, cha cha—I had a partner for each. Soon there would be a Mixer dance where partners were changed at the sound of a whistle. A drum roll heralded an announcement,

"O.K. everyone! Gotta have a parade of all you costumed guys so we can give prizes! Some of you look pretty scary tonight. Get in a circle now and strut your stuff!"

As I joined the circle, looking first to the right, then to the left to assess the costumes, my eyes rested on a new face, a man wearing a T-shirt with *BARISHNIKOV* emblazoned across the front. A silhouetted figure of a ballet dancer just below left no doubt of the T-shirt's statement. Well, I thought, there's someone who knows about ballet. That's intriguing. I hope I get to dance with him. I'll let him know *I* know who Baryshnikov is. That's more than most folks here would recognize. This new fellow had an engaging grin, though I didn't think him particularly handsome. But he was trim and not too tall, or too short.

When the mixer started, the whistle blew several times before I found myself standing in front of the stranger. He smilingly held out his arms, muscular and sure. We moved quickly into the rhythms of a brisk foxtrot.

"I'm Juliana. What's your name?" Time was short,

"Rich," he said, "Because I'm not." Then he laughed and added, "Real name's Emil, Emil Richmond but nobody can pronounce Emil right so I go by Rich."

"I like Baryshnikov's dancing." I managed to say just as the whistle blew again.

"Thanks for the dance," Rich said as he turned to another woman.

After that evening, whenever Rich arrived at a dance,

I maneuvered to a position within his eyesight. As time went on, my welcoming smile soon led to many dances together, both of us enjoying our mutual love of the movement and the music. There was something about his ready laugh, and the small bits of conversation we managed during whirling turns and breathless swings that kept me interested. Rich was an excellent dancer, and he assured me many times—

"You can follow anything! " while I basked in his approval.

One evening he said as we walked to our separate cars in the parking lot at the end of the evening, "We ought to get better acquainted. Would you like to have dinner with me some evening?"

Would I! We arranged a date for the following Tuesday, and I drove home singing *As Time Goes By* aloud, over and over.

Rich brought me two books on that first date, one a John Cheever volume of short stories, the other a Sierra Club publication. He could not have pleased me more, for I felt he recognized a side of me that wasn't apparent on the dance floor. We talked for hours over dinner and were amazed at the commonality of our interests. The Sierra Club for instance, which he had belonged to for more years than I had. I learned too that he'd lived mostly in southern California where he still owned a house in Riverside. He'd had a business there for many years. He told me about his two children, a son and daughter, whose mother, his first wife, had died when they were eight and four. He had married again, a schoolteacher named Bernice. But they had grown apart.

"She just didn't want to do the things I did, once the kids were through school, so I finally moved up to San Francisco. Thought I'd make a fresh start, maybe end up in Alaska. She's still in the house. We're friends. We've never gotten divorced, no real need to, but it's been years since we've lived together as man and wife."

I understood. I had just recently served divorce papers on Jim; it would be six months or so before our status was final. It's easy to procrastinate when there is no pressing need to do otherwise.

Rich and I had many more areas in common. We both loved to read, to hike and camp, go to movies and plays: one subject always led to another. I thought of Mother and Dad, sitting at the kitchen table late at night, talking and laughing with one another. I'd wished for that kind of companionship all through my marriage with Jim. Maybe life was going to bring me some of that joy...

There were likes and dislikes too.

"I hate to travel," Rich said one day. "It's uncomfortable I can learn all I need to know about the world in the National Geographic, sitting in my chair at home".

"Oh I love the adventure of going to new places, seeing the architecture, smelling the smells. Who needs an armchair?"

He hated Opera; I was currently dating a fellow Sierra Club hiker who'd bought season tickets for the two of us for the San Francisco Opera season, though I had to admit I hadn't exactly formed a passion for the art form.

Rich disliked Beethoven; loved Bach. I loved the passion of Beethoven, thought Bach repetitious.

Our friendship progressed through the next few weeks. Rich drove regularly from his office in San Francisco to Santa Clara, just to be with me. The combination home/office of his Business Broker firm was in a large upstairs apartment In South San Francisco on Ocean Avenue. He loved his new life, the one with me in it. He loved me.

I was falling in love too. His visits were full of surprises: a fresh loaf of bread, a poem he'd written for me, a new joke. I loved his laugh, his lack of pretense. We met each other's children, learned to know them, compared grandchildren.

A year after I met Rich, I bought a condo in Santa Clara. It was time for me to own something: I didn't like paying rent. I scraped enough money together from my just-finalized divorce settlement to make a down payment, and moved into a two bedroom, two-bath unit, surrounded by lush lawns and large magnolia trees.

"Why didn't you let me buy it for you?" Rich asked, when I told him of my purchase. I made some excuse, but the truth was I didn't want to share my ownership with anyone. This was the first home I alone had owned: my freedom had come at too great a price to give it up quickly. I reveled in decorating it, with the help of my sister-in-law, Helen, my brother Bob's wife. Together we combed furniture stores, selected colors, incorporated what I already possessed to make a charming home. I could walk to work and back. I could swim in the morning in the pool just outside my front door. Life was good! I invited friends to visit, play bridge, and share meals. Rich often spent the weekend, taking me to brunch and tea dancing whenever possible. The women at work, most of them years younger than myself, remarked on how happy I looked, saying,

"I don't know how you do it, Juliana—working all day and dancing at night. I'm exhausted when I go home after work." I just smiled.

It was inevitable that Rich would move in with me, though somehow I hadn't thought it would be so soon—just a few months after I'd taken possession of my new home. On the Saturday that he began moving clothes into the spare closet, I developed a bruising headache. Somehow I'd not realized he was moving in so soon. I'd wanted us to live together; knew it would happen sometime. But not today!

But today it was, and as the weekend wore on, my headache disappeared. Rich was fun to have around! He sang a lot, and I, who couldn't carry a tune, loved hearing the familiar songs. He often laughed aloud when reading the paper or *The New Yorker*, calling me to share the joke with him. I still come across part of a little poem I wrote to him once—

Do you know how precious a gift
Is the sound of your laughter, booming.

He found office space a few blocks from our home; had new stationary printed and settled in. Kahn's, the small department store in San Francisco's Mission district that Rich had bought as an investment the year before, demanded more time than he liked, and he had to make many trips there to give advice to the manager he'd hired to run the store.

Rich had proposed when he moved in with me, "We'll live together and share everything as long as you like. I don't think we need to get married, but if you want to, I will divorce Bernice immediately and we'll have a wedding."

I agreed to wait. I thought it a good idea to see how comfortable we were together over time. As the months went by, I realized more and more how compatible we were and one day in early spring I told him,

"Honey, I don't want us just to live together. I want to be married."

"Okay," he said, and began the process of divorcing Bernice the next week. My brother, Bob, an attorney in San Jose, handled the details for him and at the end of summer, on September 19, 1981, Rich and I were married in the lovely garden of dear friends. It was one of the happiest days of my life, and I never regretted my decision to marry once again.

CHALLENGE

I'd always wondered, somewhere in my being, if I could measure up to a real life challenge. By that I meant facing a terminal illness or something dreadful happening to someone I loved. In spite of earlier difficulties in my life, I felt I'd been very lucky overall, and part of me wondered if I was soft; would cave in when disaster hit.

I got a chance to find out in 1988, when Rich, my beloved husband of seven years, came home from a business call one day, saying he felt "funny, oh so funny" and collapsed on the sofa. Hours later, in the Emergency room at Kaiser Hospital, a doctor came to me with X-rays in his hand.

"Your husband has a blood clot in his brain—see here"—he showed me the pictures, pointing out the clot area. It looked like a Rorschach blot test: or the wings of a black butterfly. "He's going to need immediate surgery. You should know he might not recover from it. We're sending him to the Redwood City location where they specialize in this sort of thing."

I prayed all the way to the hospital, as daughter Cathryn drove,—please God, let Rich live. But let him die if he's going to be a complete invalid. That's what he'd want. But please—let him live!

I didn't know, during the long hours that Cathy and Lewis, Rich's son, and I waited in the deserted patients' lounge, that my prayers had been answered. It took the exhausted appearing surgeon to give me the news.

"Your husband is fine, Mrs. Richmond. He came through the surgery nicely. He will be paralyzed on his right side for a while, but that will pass. The clot shut off blood to the speech center of his brain, though, and he'll have a lot more trouble with that."

I was so relieved and happy to have Rich alive and, after a few months, completely mobile, that I felt equal to any challenge. After all, we could still laugh together at his clumsy attempts to eat with wooden splints on his fingers to keep them straight, or at his struggles to say his name. Surely he would recover his speech in due time! I did not see immediately that a real sea change in our lives had taken place because of the stroke: that we would never be the same again. What Rich had been left with was called Wernicke's Aphasia:

> "The aphasia syndrome, as described by Wernicke in 1908, consists of loss of comprehension of spoken language, loss of ability to read (silently) and write, and distortion of articulate speech. Hearing is intact. The affected persons may speak fluently with a natural language rhythm, but the result has neither understandable meaning nor syntax. Despite the loss of comprehension, the word memory is preserved and words are often chosen correctly."

Challenges

Sometimes coping with answered prayers is difficult.

Twenty questions had never been one of my favorite games, but it became a daily, hourly, sometimes minute by minute, ritual in which I struggled to figure out what Rich was trying to say. I tried to be patient. I was patient, but often angry and frustrated as well, shouting "I don't know what you mean!" when a soft answer would have been better; wishing the whole situation would go away when I knew it wouldn't.

Rich was struggling too, trying to be understood. Sometimes he resorted to sign language——"You know, him, over *there!*" pointing his full arm in an easterly direction.

"Oh, you mean *Leo!*" I'd guess, remembering his dear friend who lived in Philadelphia. And then we would laugh in relief, hug each other until something else he wanted to say eluded me.

Fortunately, Rich had been a talker before the stroke, and I knew many of his thoughts and attitudes enough to interpret fairly well. That habit did not cease with the stroke. Unlike many in his position who found it difficult to communicate and gradually stopped trying, Rich talked and talked: I listened and tried to translate. Often we laughed over some of my interpretations of his garbled words, but many times we glared at one another in frustration.

I took Rich to countless sessions with his speech therapist, Rosemary Berwald who was infinitely kind and patient with him, smiling gently as he tried to pronounce words that eluded him. Frequently the three of us laughed together at Rich's mistakes. We cracked up the day he rendered "Happy Birthday to You" singing the entire verse in numerals—*one, two, three, four, five, six!* in perfect tune and timing. He good-naturedly joined in the laughter; not realizing exactly what was funny, but willing to go along with our fun. In his "homework" sessions though, in which I tried to help, he wore out after fifteen or twenty minutes.

At the end of a couple of years, it was apparent that Rich had progressed as far as he was capable of doing. We stopped the speech therapy sessions.

I learned to accept what was.

The language difficulties, coupled with business worries over the small department store in San Francisco Rich had bought in 1980, wore me out. It was up to me to keep the store running, though I didn't have to be there in person. I became familiar with ordering supplies, figuring if the cash flow was sufficient to cover their cost (often it wasn't) and filling out Board of Equalization forms as well as the thousand other details of running a business. There was barely enough income to pay salaries to Gertrude and Bayardo, the trusted couple who ran the store on a day-to-day basis.

There were times when I thought that nightmare would never end, and nights when sleep eluded me as I pondered the solutions to business problems: What if Bayardo got sick (he had no health insurance and had high blood pressure). What if Gertrude needed an operation? I worried about them as I would my own family.

Of course it did all end, when the store was finally sold after four or five years. Now I can look back and be grateful for the experience. It taught me the value of good and loyal people whom I could trust, and it certainly gave me more empathy for the anxieties of a small business owner. I had never fully realized before how interdependent a businessman and his employees are.

It was humor and love that got me—us—through the next six years.

Humor and love and a sense that I had to take care of myself in order to care for Rich. I did that by sticking to my swimming routine and getting out with friends from time to time. Though Rich couldn't communicate well, he could still dance. We continued going to our beloved *Debonair Dancers* and other places. Amazingly, he could play bridge even if he couldn't do more than point at a logo card I made to show what suit he wanted to bid. So we were not without friends, wonderful friends who listened patiently and tried to understand what Rich was struggling to say.

Most importantly to me, I began to write about our experience in a class I was attending. The writing helped to objectify the trials and frustrations and gave me a focus other than myself. Sharing the writing with a class was a tremendous support. In fact, I've often found that writing down a problem, putting it in clear and precise terms has helped me find my way out of it.

Then, in the spring of 1991, Rich was diagnosed with lung cancer—he who had never smoked in his life—and three years later he was gone.

Those were tough times, but again my stubborn faith that things would get better; the knowledge that I was doing the best I could under difficult circumstances, got me through. Sometimes I even felt proud of myself that I'd maintained my "cool" and thanked God for Rich's sweet nature and sense of humor.

———————

I have never lost the conviction that life is a gift, given only once, and that I must cherish that gift and make the most of it no matter what the circumstances.

Roses

On a May Saturday afternoon in 1990 my three daughters and I sat together at lunch. We were in Cathy's newly redecorated townhouse, done in sharp contrasts of black and white, punctuated by colorful Picasso prints on the walls. The tone of our gathering was mellow, reminiscent, no doubt abetted by the Chardonnay we sipped as we ate pasta salad fragrant with mild spring onions and Balsamic vinegar.

It was my Mother's Day celebration, a time to savor the triumphs of the past year:

I felt peaceful, a triumph in itself. Right now the family was fine. Right now there was relative peace in the world for the first time in decades. Today was one for ignoring the small malignancies that might be taking hold; the weakened blood vessels that could erupt at any time. This was a day to reap the harvest of content that comes when your children have become adults you enjoy.

Things were better at home, too. Much of the pressure that Rich's stroke in 1988 had placed me under had lifted imperceptibly, its absence noted more by longer hours of sleep and greater freedom, than any other way. Today, for instance, I had felt no hesitancy in leaving him alone for the afternoon. Indeed, the small smile as he said goodbye told me he planned to enjoy the time in his own way, without interference. I knew the feeling. I savored the hours when he was away from home, out to lunch with a friend or playing bridge at the Senior Center. That was a time when I didn't have to try to understand his garbled speech because of the aphasia caused by the stroke; didn't have to combat the frustration I felt at the difficulty of communication. It was then I put music on the stereo, loud, or had the luxury of utter silence, the atmosphere exactly as I wanted it. Yes, I understood his smile.

I brought out snapshots from our recent cruise along the coast of Mexico, the first we'd ever taken. Heretofore, our trips had always involved effort—the chores of camping, the challenge of learning, or hiking new terrain. But a cruise! Ah, there is hedonism at its best! Despite my Protestant upbringing, I had found it delightful.

I'm beginning to sound like a typical retired elder, I thought, talking about vacations and cruises. But why not? Rich and I have found out you better do what you can, when you can. Aloud I said, in response to a query,

"Rich loved it. He played bridge every day; we danced in the evenings and ate all the wonderful food. I did too—I read a good book, and never had to wonder where he was—you can't get off a ship at sea! I did some snorkeling too.

The water was marvelous, and the fish—I felt like I was in a page of the *National Geographic!*"

I thought also about his retreats into silence when our dinner partners grew too voluble for his limited understanding and I tried to comfort him by squeezing his hand under the table. And my annoyance when he got up very early in the morning and bumbled around the small cabin, waking me prematurely, asking where's this? What did you do with—you know, I had yesterday, the, the THING! By the time I'd figured out the THING (shoes, toothbrush, sweatshirt) I was awake beyond return to sleep thinking as so often before—this is probably funny, but not right now. No point in going into that with the girls.

The conversation drifted from one daughter to another: Judy's three girls, my granddaughters Lindsey, Caron and Michelle, and their teenage escapades, Joan's work with the Coastal Conservancy, Cathy's new cat and her husband's adjustment to it.

"Mike used to hate cats, he *says* but now I catch him petting her when I'm not looking..."

We talked a little about son Jim, away in Atlanta, Georgia getting his PhD in Psychology, and what a long time it was taking.

"I miss him and his dry humor," Joan said and we all nodded.

The clock struck four and we stood to leave. I had a moment of gentle nostalgia, thinking would I ever again take for granted a time of special fun and closeness? I hoped not, though I knew better. It is very hard to be constantly mindful of all one's blessings.

As I drove home, I remembered we were scheduled to play bridge that evening with friends. How thoughtful they had all been since Rich's stroke! Waiting patiently for him to bid or to play the next card, trying so hard to understand his words as he expounded on some theory he'd formed about the universe. Who could understand that? Sometimes I wished his mind were not so far ranging. I'd never be able to repay those loyal friends for their kindness.

I thought about Rich too, as I drove: how happy he had seemed lately, more content, less frustrated in trying to pursue former business interests. Joan's gift of a jigsaw puzzle at Christmas had started him on a new hobby, and I marveled at his persistence in fitting the small pieces together. He'd done several of them since the first one. His philosophical acceptance of the turnaround in his life never ceased to amaze me.

Cherish the mood, I thought. Tomorrow may be different. There were sometimes mood swings to deal with: sudden angers, sulks, tears without warning. They didn't come often, thank goodness.

Rich stood grinning at me as I came in the door. "Have a good time?" He held out his arms for a hug.

"Oh, yes. The girls—" Ready to spill out my story, I sensed an urgency in him to tell me his. "What did you do? Was it a long afternoon for you?"

"I-I went over—you know, where I go..." he waved his arm in an easterly direction. I braced myself for the inevitable guessing game.

"Where'd you go? For a walk? To Larry's? Library?"

"No. Over there." Impatience tinged his voice. "Come. Look, I'll show you. Nice. For you, tomorrow."

Oh, Mother's Day, I thought. I was surprised he'd remembered. He seemed pleased with himself as he took my elbow, steering me into the kitchen. "Beautiful...I hope..." He opened the freezer section of the 'fridge, saying proudly, "Look. For you."

On top of the stacks of frozen food lay a bouquet of pink roses. "Over there" had been the Lucky store a half-mile away. I pictured Rich walking home in the hot sunshine, carefully shading the delicate blossoms, sniffing their perfume from time to time. He often called me to smell the roses in bloom when we went out walking. I could almost see his jaunty step as he anticipated my surprise and pleasure at this first gift he had bought since his stroke. My heart ached for the disappointment he would feel when he realized his mistake in judgment.

I lifted the ribbon-tied cellophane package and laid it gently on the countertop, as though by taking care now I could delay the inevitable, I noted the haze of frost crystals on the pink blossoms. If only I hadn't stayed so long talking, I thought. Maybe I could have gotten home before they froze. I plunged the stems into a vase of lukewarm water, thinking vaguely of frostbite remedies. Maybe they'd revive.

"Is it ok. I didn't know...couldn't remember..."

I thought of all the times Rich had watched me put roses in a vase, in water. The connection with those memories just wasn't there. How could I do anything but cherish the thought?

"They're beautiful, darling"! What a wonderful surprise!" Over his shoulder I could see the rosebuds drooping limply on their stems like tired ballet dancers.

By the next morning, Rich had made another trip to the store and replaced the now blackened roses with another bouquet, which lasted well into the following week. We admired them extravagantly each day, reveling in their delicate scent and culling out the dead ones as the days went on, until only a single bloom was left.

COPING ·

January 1994

Ihaven't sat at this computer since the day early in December when Dr. Hung told us Rich had a tumor in his chest that would probably kill him in about nine months. The strange thing is, we both accepted that diagnosis without question, though I did say are you sure you have the right X-ray? Even knowing they probably did. The doctor, looking serious, took me to the viewer where the picture still hung, illuminated with light, and I could see the name EMIL RICHMOND in the upper right-hand corner.

Since then we've gone through the holidays: writing the dread news on Christmas cards to family and friends, avoiding thoughts of what next year might be like. I put up a few lights and set out some familiar objects that herald the season for me. Rich never paid much attention to such things anyway, and for once I was grateful for his inattention.

We got through the holiday: Christmas Eve at Judy's, the festive day at my brother Paul's and his wife Cici's home, when Rich was in such good spirits he insisted on dancing with Cici and Joan. Draining a liter of fluid from his lungs the day before had helped his energy level. I felt as though an invisible glass wall separated me from a reality I hadn't quite faced up to, and the somewhat strained but fairly easy small talk, very light and good natured, helped. It all went rather well, with Rich's cavalier attitude toward approaching death putting everyone pretty much at ease.

He had always been very philosophical about the large issues of life— God, love, money, friendship, and death. I didn't even want to cry when Rich and I were together. The time seemed too precious to waste on grieving.

We seem to be taking this new shocking development in stride. I'm not trying to hide feelings from Rich, but I'm not fostering negative ones either. We pretend normalcy, measuring the days by the tasks to be done. Each morning, except for weekends, we leave the house at 9:10 to be at O'Connor Hospital for his radiation treatment. Rich holds my arm as we descend the stairs carefully, I very conscious of keeping a sure footing for us both. Last week his breathing was so labored, and he was so weak and tired, with his stomach aching severely early in the mornings, that I wondered if the treatments were killing him. If it would be better to just stop everything and let the process of the disease go forward. But after Friday, when Dr. Dailey took two quarts of fluid from Rich's chest, and he could breathe again without having the sound carry from one room to another, we both took a little hope.

"The tumor looks a little smaller," the doctor said, holding the X-ray up to the light for me to see, after he'd drawn out the coffee colored fluid that filled the glass jars on the floor of the hospital procedure room. "Keep on with the radiation—it seems to be working. Maybe he won't build up so much fluid again."

I took Rich home at five o'clock and we ate the lentil soup I'd made earlier in the week. We've been eating lots of soups and stews; nourishing, easy to swallow meals that Rich downs with dedication, if not gusto. He can only hold small amounts and I cheer him on, as though he'd made a touchdown when he manages to eat a full plate of food.

He slept fourteen hours straight when he went to bed that Friday, and I got in about ten of uninterrupted slumber. He'd been up and down during the night for weeks, sleeping fitfully and spending much of the time dozing in a chair in the living room, wrapped in a warm afghan. Sometimes he'd call me in pain with his aching stomach, and I'd urge him to eat a piece of Melba toast, sip a glass of milk, take an antacid. He'd gradually nod off, or go back to bed and I would drink a small glass of vodka and orange juice to calm myself and read until sleep came again. One morning I was so exhausted I was cross with Rich, and then felt guilty, apologizing profusely.

Today has been better. We slept well last night, and visitors last evening raised our morale. There was time to give Rich a bath, since his treatment had been moved to two o'clock in the afternoon for today only—something about a routine check on the X-ray machine. Even though it was raining a little, I went for my thrice-weekly swim at the International Swim Center in Santa Clara while Rich napped. A man I often see entering the pool area as I leave, and who always greets me with "How's the water today?"

smiled at me as I walked out to the car, and said,

"You don't let anything stop you, do you?" and I thought *if you only knew. I'm swimming for my life.*

I'm beginning to know some of the people who come to the O'Connor Radiology department for treatment when we do. While Rich is changing into the peach colored cotton top that refuses to stay closed and hangs on his thin shoulders like a draped dishtowel, I sit in the waiting room where other patients and their escorts wait. Some days I don't want to greet anyone, the tears are too close for speech. It's a time when I can weep unobserved by Rich. But other days, especially when plump, jolly Tony with three tumors on his spine is there, greetings are appropriate, even unavoidable.

"Good morning!" booms Tony. "How're ya doin' today?" He lowers himself into a straight-backed chair carefully. His left hand is nearly useless, the result he's told me, of the tumor's affect on the nerves in his upper back.

"First I knew I had a problem, when that happened," he said. "So they're doing radiation for that one—six weeks— and then chemo for the other two. Guess I'm lucky to have such good treatment."

I wonder to myself how the chemotherapy can be separated out for the different locations, if there are two kinds of cancers present. But Tony is not the worrying kind, at least not outwardly.

"I'm going to have a great day," he says. "Wife and I are goin' to San Francisco to see *The Phantom of the Opera* I've had the tickets for months"

"Oh, I saw that! It's wonderful—you'll love it," says Irene, a tall gray-haired woman who marches with military steps into the treatment room when her name is called. Lipsticked and with hair neatly combed, she smiles easily at me and has told me a little of her history.

"Breast cancer, lumpectomy," she said one morning. "This is just a precautionary treatment." I assure her I have a friend who had such an incident fifteen years ago and is staggeringly healthy today. I push away the thought that the same friend's husband died of lung cancer two years ago. But he was a smoker. This shouldn't be happening to Rich!

The last few days a new woman has joined our group. Tall and slender, with smartly coiffed ash-blonde hair, she strides into the waiting room and sinks into the couch. She neither smiles nor looks at anyone; hides her face behind a magazine. *Leave me alone!* her demeanor shouts. I wonder how long her anger will last and if I'll see a different side of her before Rich finishes his treatments.

In this battleground against death, the attendants are exceedingly cheerful. "How're ya' doing, sweetheart," says Vicki with a wide grin as she cradles Rich's elbow and steadies him for the walk to the big, cold table where the X-rays aware directed.

The head nurse smiles broadly at us as we enter on a Monday.

"Mr. Richmond! Did you have a good weekend?" Rich smiles back at her, not replying, and I think, *Thank God for football and the 49ers. We'd never make it through the weekends if we didn't have those games to watch and talk about!*

Three and a half years later, almost exactly to the date of Rich's death in March of 1994, I can read this account without the tears, but I can still smell the mixture of hospital odors in that radiology waiting room. A feeling of deep sadness comes over me as I remember the brave and determined spirit Rich maintained during that awful time. Every day, he told me he loved me: that I was a wonderful woman and he'd been so happy with me. I in turn, assured him of my love and gratitude for the years we'd had together. We bolstered one another as best we could.

When the end came, after more treatment, hospital stays, pain, I held Rich in my arms as he took his last breath. He was comatose then; we didn't know what he heard or understood. I knew by his irregular breathing that the end was near. "It's o.k. to go darling. I love you," I whispered. There were no more breaths.

"He's gone," the Hospice aid, who had just finished bathing Rich, said softly. I held his warm body in my arms a few minutes and then left the room, grateful that he was out of his pain and I not yet fully aware of mine.

RECOVERY

1995

I stood in front of the full-length mirror, turning my body as far left as it would go. Was the slit in the back of my skirt in the middle? Did my slip show through it? I shifted the short under slip an inch to the right—there, everything was lined up. Was my dress too short—it was a good three inches above my knees. Would it move with the long steps of the tango and waltz? I took a few experimental strides, twirled to see the effect. It was fine, no binding. My legs were good, still slim. Nylon stockings gave them a smooth, tanned look and concealed a varicose vein. I remembered the fashion commentator once at a style show for "Mature" women, who said brightly,

"Remember, ladies, the legs are the last to go! Make the most of them!"

I smiled to myself, slipping on the top of my two-piece yellow dress, which fit loosely and stylishly. The short skirt pulled easily over my hips and thighs—nice. I slipped on a pair of comfortable bone-colored pumps and eyed myself in the mirror. Not bad for a seventy four year old, I thought.

Now the makeup. It was amazing what a little eye shadow, a bit of eyeliner could do in the evening when the lights were low. Wrinkles faded; sagging skin disappeared in the shadows. I used to have a flawless, smooth complexion, one I took for granted, but that had changed. Even so, I felt like a Princess, ready for the Ball, but with no Prince Charming to escort me. Well, I could provide my own carriage.

I slid carefully into the front seat of my car, the new one I'd bought last summer, straightening my skirt so it wouldn't wrinkle, moving carefully so my new white coat would stay clean. I fastened the seat belt, started the engine. Terri Gross was interviewing someone about the Ebola virus on the radio. I changed to a music station. Enough with Ebola, I thought. I knew about that. Tonight I'd dance and forget Bosnia and the Republicans, what they were trying to do to PBS by taking funds away.

In the years when I was married to Jim, yearning to dance, to have fun, only to be met with his lack of enthusiasm, his need for a drink to "relax", followed by several more, I often turned on some catchy music and slid around our polished hardwood floors with a child in my arms, losing my everyday world in the smooth romance of a waltz or twirling rapidly to a swing number.

I'd tried to leave home early enough that Spring evening to get a parking place near the Senior Center where the ballroom was, but as I approached, I saw that others had beaten me to it. Undeterred, I found a space on the street and walked briskly down the sidewalk. I'd done that plenty of times since I started dancing again without Rich last summer, six months after he died.

It was different when I first began dancing again after Jim and I divorced. Then, I didn't know anyone except another single woman I'd met in a counseling group who went with me. I'll never forget the feeling of loneliness and rejection I often got as I sat out a dance while others swirled around the floor, laughing, their bodies moving in rhythm to the music. But in time, I got a few favorite partners and could only look in sympathy at the other women who sat along the edges of the room with fixed smiles on their faces while I glided by. I met Rich at the YMCA in Palo Alto on a Halloween night when we both were in costume, and from that night on I always had a partner that I loved to be with. I thought I'd always have him; that we'd dance into old age together, gradually stopping the activity through mutual consent. I didn't bargain on the cancer that took him away so soon.

I thought of the night last summer when I began to dance again. Rich had died in March—over a year ago now—and my friend Phyllis had urged me to join her at the Senior Center where they danced on Thursday nights. I probably wouldn't have ventured out, if it weren't for her encouragement. Until then I hadn't even dared to put dance music tapes on my stereo player for fear of the emotional storm I knew would come. But I had waltzed briefly with my brother at his son's wedding a few weeks before and we had laughed in memory of the high school days when we practiced steps in the living room together. The ice was broken, and I thought why not? Rich would understand.

But oh, to go in alone, after all the happy times when we'd walked hand in hand toward beckoning music, smiling at each other in anticipation of a good time. Could I do it? That first night, my steps were slow as I entered the hall, vowing to leave if need be, if the emotions became too acute. As I walked along the sidewalk, I met another woman entering at the same time,

"Hello," she said. "Are you new?"

"Well, sort of. I used to come here with my husband, but I haven't been in a year or so. He died in March, and this is my first time…" I felt my voice catch, and stopped.

"I know how it is," she said. "I lost my husband two years ago. We always danced too. But you can't stay home and watch TV forever. You just have to make yourself do it. My name's Delores. You can sit with me if you like."

I was relieved to have someone to sit with, since Phyllis wouldn't be there until later, and Delores and I sat together on the chairs along the wall, along with all the other waiting ladies. Soon Delores was dancing, and then an old acquaintance offered me his hand in the traditional invitation. I moved stiffly to his steps, hating the newness, longing for the feel of Rich's body against mine, his rhythm to match my own. I could barely wait for the music to stop and when it did, mumbled a "thank you" and made my way blindly into the women's bathroom where I shut myself in a cubicle. Tears spurted from my eyes; my body bent in upon itself as though I'd been kicked in the stomach. It's too much! I thought. I can't do it!

But the tears had vented my emotions somewhat. I'd stay a little longer—I didn't want to disappoint Phyllis when she arrived. I sat down beside my new friend again, and suddenly another man appeared. Dear fat bellied George with his wide smile and kind manner. Rich had

always liked him. He had dated a friend of mine for years
and we'd often seen them at dances.

"Juliana! Want to waltz?"

This time it was easier and George was full of advice.
"It's hard, I know. But you've got to get out and circulate.
You're good —when the fellows find out, you won't have
any trouble finding partners." He twirled me expertly, did
a small dip and the music stopped. "Don't be afraid to ask
the men to dance. That's the way they do it nowadays. And
for heaven's sake, take off your wedding rings!"

That was the beginning of my recovery. As always, dance
steps had led me back into life, and I had made new friends
in the process. I'd done other things also, to bring my life
into the outside world after the years I'd spent helping Rich
recover from a stroke and then nursing him through his
final illness. I'd become a docent at the San Jose Museum
of Art and taken on the presidency of the Santa Clara
Triton Museum's auxiliary. I'd traveled to Alaska, Turkey
and Thailand. I still swam regularly. But dance night at the
Senior Center continued to be a highlight in my week.

My family was somewhat scattered during this time.
Two of my daughters, Judy and Joan, lived near enough for
me to see them on a regular basis. Judy had recently retired
from years of teaching and was herself recovering from
the death of her third husband, as well as a traumatizing
surgery for a benign tumor on her auditory nerve which
had left her with a hearing loss and some facial paralysis.

Joan spent an occasional overnight with me when she
was on a business trip. I could count on her to host special
holiday family gatherings.

Cathy and Mike had moved to Austin, Texas, but were

frequent visitors to San Jose. Son Jim was still in Atlanta, completing his PhD. Though he had never married, his long time companion, Norma, was a steadfast help to him. I managed visits to him by taking Elderhostel trips to Atlanta and staying extra days to spend time with him.

Rich's two children, Anna and Lew, were always careful to invite me for Thanksgiving dinners, or special family times, which I loved attending.

My three granddaughters—Judy's children—were sweet and loving, but full of their own struggles with school and early jobs, so their visits were infrequent.

Yes, I was well nurtured. But I found myself longing to find love again—to have someone to care about and be a companion to. Would that ever happen for me again? Time was marching on and I didn't want to go dancing alone forever!

BERT

I hadn't paid any attention to the tall, slightly stooped, white haired man until we danced together. He was surprisingly smooth, though why I was surprised I can't say now.

It was a "mixer" dance, one where partners were chosen at the random commands of the person at the mike, "Men—take two steps to the middle of the circle— turn to your left and walk till I tell you to stop!"

The idea being, of course, that the woman you stopped in front of was your partner for the next two minutes. There were variations on this theme, naturally, but that's the general idea.

I liked the mixer dances. It was a chance to meet new partners; to see what impression I wanted to leave with them, or to learn something about the other. I liked the challenge of following the steps of different partners, though sometimes that was impossible when they had no sense of rhythm, rare as that was. I had secret nicknames for some of the men.

There was "Cuddles" who always wanted to press me too close and I spent an inordinate amount of energy trying to keep my distance. There was "the Shuffler," because that's all he ever did to any beat, fast or slow. Then there was the " wanna be" Fred Astaire who made up his own elaborate steps, flinging his partner wildly out and reeling her in again like a trout on a hook. You get the picture.

And there were the really good dancers—the ones you hoped the command to change would put directly in front of you. The whole mixer was worth the game when a good partner came your way and ended the two minutes by saying, "You're a beautiful dancer!" to me. Or some such remark. Aren't we all a little vain, a little still the teenagers we once were when approval was so important?

But here was this new partner and all I had was two minutes to find out something about him. I'd begun to notice his startlingly blue eyes.

"Hi - I'm Juliana."

"Bert—Bert Altmann. With two n's."

I tried to digest that. What difference did the spelling make? He's probably one of those engineer types who want everything just so. The time was nearly up—

"Have you got the foxtrot in the next set? No? Good, I'll meet you for that."

When we danced again, I thought I'd test him a little. So I told him about being a Docent at the San Jose Art museum and mentioned an article I'd just read in the *New Yorker* that had stayed in my mind. If he didn't seem to register any of that, I knew he'd only be useful for dancing, nothing more. Most men I met at these affairs would draw a blank on those subjects.

"I like to paint some myself," Bert said. "I've been working on a composition of daisies spilling out of a blue vase but I can't seem to get it right."

Well, I thought, this might prove interesting.

The first time Bert and I went out together was to have dinner at a nice restaurant. I don't remember what we ate, but we sure did talk!

"I'm a widower," he said, "and I've got five children: Two boys, three girls. They're all married—one lives in Paris with his wife and two boys—but the rest are pretty much local. Except Barbara, the youngest. She isn't married. She's got Down's syndrome and she's living with me right now, but that'll change. She's lived independently before and we're just waiting for an opportunity that's in the offing to work out."

I remembered a family on our street in Campbell who'd sent their mongoloid son to an institution when they were not able to cope. They had always seemed a little apologetic. I liked Bert's matter of fact approach and acceptance of Barbara's condition. It must have been really difficult in the beginning, when she was first born, I thought. Barbara is probably easier to get along with than the boy I knew about.

Our talk went on for hours, until the hovering waiter made Bert look at his watch. We left, to continue the conversation at my house.

"I could talk with you all night," Bert said, kissing me lightly as he left. "I'll call you tomorrow."

In the days and months that followed, Bert and I found compatibility in more than dancing. We camped at Big Sur; hiked with the Sierra Club group I belonged to, met each other's families. Bert was seven months older than I. He'd been raised in Ohio where his father was a college professor. We seemed to speak the same language: we were comfortable together.

At Christmas, my daughter Joan bought Bert a special bottle of Port wine.

"You didn't need to do that, honey,"

"I just wanted to Mom. I like the guy!" I did, too.

We took a trip together, to Turkey and the Greek Islands and on the way home stopped in Paris for a visit with Bert's son Scott and his family. Now I'd met them all, and liked them. They seemed to like me too.

It wasn't long before we began to talk of living together.

"You could rent your condo and move in with me," Bert said one day. "I could help you move and get it ready."

It took a few months for me to decide to leave my comfortable home, but in October of 1998 that is what I did.

The arrangement has worked out wonderfully well. Bert and I have a quiet, loving companionship that is perfect for this stage of our lives. I love this house, which Bert built himself at about the same time Jim and I were building ours in Campbell. Its Spanish style adobe structure nestles in the hills above the town of Los Gatos, close enough to walk to, and far enough away to afford a lovely view.

The home we've made together is a welcoming place for family and friends. We particularly like to entertain on the spacious deck on warm summer evenings when the lights of the town spread out like a sparkling golden ribbon below. And we have enough room to practice our dance steps and to hang our collection of paintings!

We've continued to travel and dance (Bert is as fond

of our Debonair Dancers as Rich was. In fact, he was President of the group for three years). Sometimes we take painting classes together, but Bert doesn't write stories, or play bridge. After all, you have to have *some* separate pastimes to keep a relationship in balance!

Morning Walk

Iwake at 6 a.m. on this Tuesday morning and lie in bed for half an hour reviewing my dreams and the day ahead. At 6:30 I creep out of bed so as not to disturb Bert whose idea of early morning begins at 8:00 a.m. But I've peeked out the window and the sun is shining and I can't wait to get out into the fresh air.

At 7:05 I'm walking, earplugs of my Sony Walkman tucked securely in, and on my way to Graceland. My currently favorite singer, Paul Simon, is taking the walk with me this morning and I look forward to his company. People have said to me "I don't want to hear anything but the birds when I walk and I want to see everything along the way."

I think smugly that I can hear the birds too above the soft sound I permit myself and also the autos that swish up and down our so-called country road. I keep my path close to the side of the road, knowing the drivers can see me but not pushing my luck by straying toward the middle. Paul is singing *Graceland, Graceland, we're on our way to Graceland* and I strive to find the beat as I walk. I'd really like to dance to the music, but there's a limit to what kind of a picture I want to present to the world even at this early hour. After all, some of those drivers maybe aren't quite awake yet and the sight of an old lady in hiking shoes bopping along the road might unnerve them for the day!

I'm walking fast now, in time to the beat of *Diamonds on the Soles of her Shoes*. The daffodils on the side of the road catch the early morning light on their petals—diamonds enough for me this morning. A fountain swishes its watery cargo from the pile of rocks to the bottom of its path and I think of Yosemite and Vernal Falls in miniature.

I Don't Want No Part of This Crazy Love Paul sings and I think I've had those crazy loves in my life, mostly when I was a teenager or feeling like one. I don't want to think about that on this lovely day. I just want to walk and smell the piece of lavender I've skinned from its stem as I passed a bed of the fragrant flowers. I just want to feast my eyes on the fresh greens and delicate pinks of spring.

I'm at the end of my mile trek. Its time to turn back and retrace my steps home. It's an uphill route going back, so I'll be getting some aerobic exercise. The tape turns too after several moments of silence, then Paul comes back into my world with *You Can Call Me Al* and I try to hum along with him, but my early morning fog-filled croak stops me. I'll sing in my head, I think and I wave hello to two women who are walking and talking together. I get more nature from a walk with Paul than I would with a friend!

I'm home again at 7:40 and Bert is, to my surprise, up and staring vaguely at the coffee pot and spilling beans into the burr grinder. I know it would be simpler to buy the coffee already ground and just measure it out, but its more fun to grind it ourselves. I think it's the best coffee we can make. I fill the carafe up to the six-cup mark, and Bert carefully pours it into the well of the coffee maker. We sit silently spooning out grapefruit wedges with our triangular shaped grapefruit spoons and listen to the water bubbling its way through the filter and into the pot. A wonderful smell fills the air; the morning paper rustles in our hands and soon the sound of cereal spoons against the side of the dish will fill the silence. I don't like a lot of noise in the morning, and neither does Bert, though we occasionally remark on a story in the paper. The headlines are full of news of war; too dreadful to talk about. I look out the window at our lovely view across the valley to the Santa Cruz mountain range. Los Gatos rooftops dot the town's location in the valley below. St. Mary's church tower cuts the sky. Our day is beginning.

Since I began living with Bert eight years ago, life has been more tranquil than at any other time in my life. Bert is the companion and "best friend" of these years that is exactly what I've needed, and whether we are dancing, walking or reading together, I am at peace. (Well, except for the times we argue about the best way to perform a dance step, that is) He is an easy, thoughtful, fun-loving man who takes events like new stents in his heart arteries or a stolen wallet on a trip to a foreign country pretty much in his stride.

Jim Cardellino used to say that about me "you take everything in stride" while I just thought I was doing what needed doing, in spite of inner doubts and fears.

As I think back over my life, I realize I have indeed taken a lot in stride. But don't we all—without taking in stride the challenges and crisis of our lives, what kind of lives would we have? Sometimes the decades seem like a dream, these eighty-five years of new inventions, wars, marriages, children, grandchildren, great grandchildren, homes, deaths, economic changes, travel to many countries. It has indeed been like a dance, responding to the rhythms and changing steps of life.

Writing the stories of this dream has brought them back to me, made me realize that they're all still alive within me and made me look forward to new adventures in this dance that is my life.

With Dr. Kayani at Kaiser. I'm dressed in costume for Halloween.

Rich and I, ready to dance, 1984.

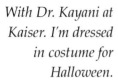

Rosemary Berwald our wonderful speech therapist and Rich, 1989.

My brothers Paul (L) and Bob (R) on my 70th birthday.

A visit to son Jim in Charleston, S.C. where he was doing "post doc" work.

Bert and I on vacation, 1998.

Enjoying morning coffee and the view, Los Gatos, 2007.

ISBN 142510385-5

9 781425 103859